THE BAGS

THE BAGS

Written by

Joel Hodgson & Nell Scovell

WRITERS' DRAFT

Printed in the United States of America

First Printing, 2021

ISBN-13: 978-1-954968-31-8 print edition
ISBN-13: 978-1-954968-32-5 ebook edition

Published by Secret Script Vault, an imprint of:

Waterside Productions

Waterside Productions
2055 Oxford Ave
Cardiff, CA 92007
www.waterside.com

For our moms
who always encouraged us not to be wasteful

Robert Hodgson
Cynthia Scovell

Editor's Note

Movies define our lives, and yet most people have never read a script for a television show or a film unless they work in the entertainment industry.

Screenwriting is a unique medium for writers. Unlike novels, a script goes through many revisions and changes before it becomes what you see on screen. Once a screenplay is written it passes into the hands of agents, directors, producers and actors. All to realize what's on the page. That process takes years.

I started working in the entertainment business as a development executive in 2005, which meant I was responsible for reading thousands of scripts, and finding great ones for our company to co-finance. Scripts that came across my desk had "attachments", which means that either actors or a director were attached to the project. Our company made films with well-known actors like *The Good Night*, *Just Friends*, and *Peaceful Warrior*. I later worked for comedian Garry Shandling.

A surprising thing that I learned was that even the most famous and beloved screenwriters and showrunners all have wonderful scripts that for whatever quirky reason, haven't found their way to the screen. (Even Garry Shandling had a comedy show that was never made that imagined God an alcoholic.)

If a script isn't produced, no one ever sees it. Understand, if the script hasn't been produced, that doesn't mean it's bad – not at all. What it usually means is it might be a misfit, or an idea that isn't in fashion, or that the writer's reps (agents and/or manager), didn't shop it or find a home for it. Writers have entire careers with only one or two scripts making it to the screen when they've written dozens. In many cases, this means that even the writer's closest friends and family might only get to see a fraction of their output.

I love misfits. I love great writing. Secret Script Vault was created to give you an experience of reading wonderful scripts you might not ever get to enjoy otherwise.

Here's How It Works

Scripts are fun and quick to read. Each page of a script represents roughly one minute of screen time. So, television scripts are about 25-30 pages, and film scripts are 90-120 pages. (In the rise of streamers, there is somewhat less adherence to these standards.) The formatting is consistent. Hundreds of people both in front of and behind the camera utilize a script in their jobs to bring the project to life.

All scripts are printed, single sided on 8.5"x11" white paper, and three-hole punched. Typically, only the top and bottom holes get a brass tack to hold the script together. (Urban legend has it that this allowed studios to reduce brass brad expenditures by one-third.) By the time a script gets to a studio, the title page may also be in color, or display the logo of the show or studio. We've intended with Secret Script Vault to replicate for you the actual experience that an actor or director has by the time the script reaches their hands. (Even the "about the book" section on the back cover is this script's "logline", which is the short summary used to define and sell the script.)

Some Terms to Know

Let's talk about scenes, which are what make up a script. Whether its horror or comedy, romance or action, scripts for the screen are written the same way.

Some things to be aware of as you read are the sluglines, also called scene headings. This is where you see:

INT./EXT.

Which stands for either INT. "interior" or EXT. "exterior". Meaning the scene is to be shot indoors or outdoors.

After that comes the place the scene is set. For example:

INT. BAKERY

You might see the words
CONTINUOUS
DAY
NIGHT
SAME
appear in the same scene heading.

INT. BAKERY - DAY

Whenever you meet a character for the first time, you'll see their name appear in ALL CAPS, often along with their age and a brief character description: CARY GRANT (30's) a debonair yet playful English gentleman.

The action lines are the description of the scene that appear briefly after the slugline.

Whenever you encounter important elements in the action lines that appear after the scene heading those will usually be in ALL CAPS, like sound effects, props, and other details, including character POV – point of view, or CU – close up. Sometimes a writer will just encourage the director to choose a NEW ANGLE.

Trends in screenwriting have evolved over the years. Now many writers choose to bold their sluglines. Others have kept the ALL CAPS for sound effects and VFX (visual effects), but dropped them for props. Also, every country has their own norms, and what you might see in a script in Canada or England will be slightly different than what you see in the United States.

Unless you're in the industry, or in film school, it's rare to read a script. Only the finished shooting scripts of well-known films or shows find their way to publication.

What stands true is that great writing is undeniable, timeless and entertaining, in every medium.

We hope that you enjoy these special scripts from Secret Script Vault: *The Greatest Shows You've Never Seen.*

Kaia Alexander

Founder, Secret Script Vault
California, 2021

Preface
By Nell Scovell

In the mid-1990s, Joel Hodgson and I teamed up to write movies for Disney. We co-wrote a credited screenplay for *Honey, We Shrunk Ourselves*, the third installment of that franchise, and an uncredited rewrite of *George of the Jungle*. One weekend afternoon, Joel pitched me an idea he had for a horror film about garbage bags that come to life and smother people. I was in before he finished his pitch which was both hilarious and socially conscious.

Joel and I kept our day jobs. I was writing on the sitcom *Coach* and he was developing *The X-Box is Turning*. On the weekends, we got together and wrote *The Bags*. It was a labor of love. We wanted to make a movie that combined the seriousness of environmental concerns with silly jokes. (I don't know which of us came up with the idea of a giant Claes Oldenburg garbage bag/art installation for the movie's climax, but the fact that it's in there means we both heartily approved.)

Our creative talents were complementary. Joel is a master of visual storytelling. All those years dissecting B-movies at *Mystery Science Theater 3000* make Joel an expert on tropes of the genre. My main focus was dialogue and character. We wanted the movie to be funny and scary similar in tone to *Tremors*. We wrote the script quickly and then revised until it was ready to be shown to the world.

I sent *The Bags* to my agent at CAA. The spec screenplay market was hot and Joel and I fantasized about selling the movie for six figures. We talked about Joel directing the movie. We made lists of casting ideas. The agents read it over the weekend and an assistant called to set up a lunch to discuss. I arrived at The Ivy, an ultra-chic restaurant in West Hollywood and joined my three agents. There was the usual small talk and eventually, I asked what they thought of *The Bags*.

"Well, I have a question," one agent said.

I figured he was going to ask, "Who do you see starring in this?" Or "Do you think you can get Claes Oldenburg?"

Instead, the agent opened his arms in exasperation and said, "Why would you write this?"

He was perplexed and now I was, too. "What do you mean?" I asked.

"Well, garbage bags just aren't scary," he replied. "We all have them in our homes."

"Exactly!" I said.

This moment of triumph was short-lived. The agents truly hated the script and refused to send it to producers.

The Bags never sold. It wasn't even read. Until now.

THE BAGS

FADE IN:

FORTY FEET BELOW THE EARTH AT THE BASE OF A LANDFILL

Panning up a CROSS SECTION of a landfill reveals *we are what we throw away*. In the discarded trash we see decades of American culture.

60's: A tattered copy of On The Road, Meet the Beatles album cover, Peter Max posters, mattress springs, space food sticks, Nancy Sinatra go-go boots, a broken cabinet TV/Stereo, Playboy magazines, milk bottles, newspapers, Life Magazine with Khrushchev on the covers, toys (Slinky, Mousetrap, Silly Putty, etc...)

70's: A tattered copy of Fear of Flying, a hot comb, a broken disco ball, Colt Malt Liquor cans, Wheaties with Mark Spitz on the box, Farrah Fawcett poster, Pampers (white), pile of aluminum pull tops, G.I. Joe with lifelike hair, discarded Libbyland dinner boxes, telephone books, Hustler Magazine, Hi-C cans, busted "Butter-up" popcorn popper.

80's: Tattered copies of a Sidney Sheldon novel, Michael Jackson album covers, soda cans with pop-tops, a broken Rubik's cube, discarded Lean Cuisine boxes, Penthouse Magazine, empty cigarette packs, half-eaten Twinkies, Chunky soup cans, turntables, more Pampers (pink and blue), panty hose, styrofoam take-out containers, busted hot-air popcorn popper.

90's: A tattered copy of "Tuesdays with Morrie," Pearl Jam cd covers, discarded Linda McCartney meatless frozen meals, more Pampers (now for swimming!), eight different brands of bottled water, an original Mac computer, busted beanie babies, microwave popcorn bags.

Moving into the new millennium, we hit a MAMMOTH LAYER OF SEALED GREEN GARBAGE BAGS. The camera moves up and out of the landfill onto:

EXT. LOVELY GRASS-COVERED PARK - DAY

The city of NEWFIELD is in the background. It's RAINING SLIGHTLY. Pan over to:

A DUMPSTER TIPPED ON ITS SIDE WITH THE LID OPEN

A STRAY DOG approaches and sniffs around the spilled garbage. As the SUN STARTS TO BREAK THROUGH, the dog digs deeper into the dumpster and finds a GREEN GARBAGE BAG. He clenches the bag firmly in his teeth and tugs it out of the dumpster.

FX: THE CLOUDS PART AND A SHAFT OF LIGHT HITS THE BAG

ABRUPTLY, THE BAG YANKS THE DOG BACK INTO THE DUMPSTER. THE DUMPSTER LID SLAMS SHUT.

SFX: THE DOG BEGINS TO WHIMPER

Lightning, thunder, rain.

SUPER: **THE BAGS**

CUT TO:

INT. SUBURBAN KITCHEN - McKENNA'S HOUSE - MORNING

TITLE CARD #1: Spring, 2001

TITLE CARD #2: Breakfast time

It's breakfast at the McKennas and Dad (EVAN) is cooking up a storm.

1. Evan cracks eggs into the bowl and tosses the shells in a trash can lined with a BRIGHT, GRASS-GREEN "CLEAN BAG."

2. Evan takes the last piece of bacon out of the package and puts it in the sizzling frying pan. He throws the package into the Clean bag.

3. Evan starts to make scrambled eggs, pouring the beaten eggs into a smaller frying pan. He spills a little egg. He reaches for the paper towels and pulls for a square. The rack keeps spinning and he winds up with a huge wad of paper towels. He cleans up the mess, then throws the clump of paper towels in the Clean bag.

4. Evan dumps the coffee grinds into the Clean bag.

5. Evan pours pulpy "fresh-squeezed" orange juice from concentrate into glasses, emptying the carton which he tosses. It banks off the wall and lands in the Clean bag.

CUT TO:

The table is a masterpiece. Evan dries his hands with a paper towel and goes to the now overflowing Clean bag. Evan drops the paper towel into the trash then flips the spring so the lid comes down.

                    EVAN
          Breakfast!

Mom (GRETCHEN) enters, dressed in a two-piece suit.

                    GRETCHEN
          Wow, look at this spread. It's
          beautiful.

                    EVAN
          And so's my wife.

They kiss. Gretchen sits and starts heaping food on his
plate. JULIE McKENNA, their pretty 17-year old daughter,
enters. She puts her hand over her nose.

                    JULIE
          I'm gonna puke. Do I smell scorched
          animal flesh?

                    GRETCHEN
          It's bacon. And you don't have to eat
          it.

                    JULIE
          I won't.

                    EVAN
          Good. More for me. I like scorched
          animal flesh.

Evan piles the bacon high on his plate.

                    JULIE
          Dad, meat is killing our planet.
          First, it's an inefficient food
          source. And second, all the cow farts
          are changing our weather patterns.

                    EVAN
          Well, let's just hope the wind isn't
          blowing in our direction.

SFX: A LOUD CRASH OUTSIDE

As everyone who has ever lived in the suburbs knows, the
GARBAGE TRUCK is on its way.

                    EVAN (CONT'D)
               (realizing)
          It's Thursday. I forgot to put out
          the trash.

                    JULIE
          I'll do it, Dad. It's okay. I can't
          stand this stenchiness any longer.

Julie stands.

                    EVAN
          Take the Clean bag. It's full.

Julie heads to the trash can and removes the Clean bag.
She seals the bag up with the patented CLICKERTOP SEALING
SYSTEM (a small, yellow, hard plastic pair of pincers
with a hinge that ratchets into place with a CLICK.)

                    GRETCHEN
          I have to admit, Evan, the
          clickertops on the Clean bags work
          better than the old plastic twists.

                    EVAN
          Thanks, honey.
               (calls out)
          See, Julie, you say I don't care
          about the environment, but your old
          dad is in charge of marketing
          Plastech's new Clean bag. And you
          know what?
               (proudly)
          They're biodegradable.

                    JULIE
          What does that mean? Instead of
          sticking around for half a million
          years, they'll break down in ten
          thousand? This bag will still last
          longer than our skeletons.

Julie grabs the Clean bag and heads out, defiantly.

EXT. STREET OUTSIDE THE MCKENNA'S HOUSE - DAY

The garbage truck is stopped at the house just up the
street from the McKenna's. DARREN, 19, sits behind the
wheel, listening to a loud ROCK SONG on his earbuds. MATT
is behind the truck, loading. He's a good-looking guy in
his early twenties and wears a weightlifter belt.

EXT. DRIVEWAY OUTSIDE THE MCKENNA HOUSE - DAY

Julie opens one of the two city-issued, heavy-plastic,
wheeled GARBAGE BINS at the top of the driveway and
deposits the new bag. She closes the lid and starts to
drag them to the curb with that familiar RUMBLE. The
driveway is steep and slick from the rain and one of the
bins RUMBLES away from Julie and STARTS TO TIP.

                    JULIE
          Oh no!

It's the classic struggle between man and garbage bin.
The lid FLIPS OPEN and some trash falls out of the top
(milk carton, paper towels, etc...) but Julie reacts
quickly. Before the bin can topple, she sticks out her
foot and stops it with her ankle. She grabs the bin and
manages to push it back upright. She continues dragging
the bin to the curb and sets it on the flat part of the
driveway. She rubs her ankle in pain.

                    JERRY
               (a friendly voice)
          Yo, Julie. How goes the battle?

Julie turns around to see her neighbor, JERRY GORDON, coming down his driveway carrying a little brown bag. He is in his forties and a hippie.

                    JULIE
          Oh, hi Jerry.

                    JERRY
          Two full bins, huh? Your family sure
          makes a lot of garbage.
               (re: the brown paper
                bag)
          This is all my trash. Everything else
          I put on the compost heap.

                    JULIE
               (pouts)
          My parents won't let me have a
          compost heap. They say fruit flies
          don't make good pets.

Jerry puts his trash neatly at the curb.

                    JERRY
          Well, don't give up the good fight.
               (makes a fist)
          Further on, friend.

ANGLE ON: THE GARBAGE TRUCK - UP THE STREET

Matt finishes working the mechanism that lifts the bins into the truck. He picks up the stray garbage that fell outside the truck then BANGS THE SIDE OF THE TRUCK.

                    MATT
               (calling out)
          Time to switch.
               (no response)
          Switch!

Darren can't hear. He's listening to the loud music. He keeps drumming on the steering wheel in time to the music. All of a sudden, Matt's head appears in the window making a scary face. Darren JUMPS.

                    DARREN
          Dude, you scared me.

Matt LAUGHS.

                    MATT
          I said, "switch."

Darren starts to get out of the truck cab.

ANGLE ON MCKENNA'S DRIVEWAY

Julie is gathering the stuff on the driveway that fell out of the bin when the garbage truck pulls up with Matt at the wheel. Darren is holding on the back of the truck and hidden from view. Matt spots Julie.

                    MATT (CONT'D)
               (from the window)
          Julie. Yo, Julie.

Julie heads to the bin to deposit the trash.

                    JULIE
               (blasé)
          Hello, Matt.

                    MATT
          Hey, a bunch of us are playing pool
          tonight, you wanna come?

                    JULIE
          Thanks, but I can't. I'm... busy.

Julie turns to head back up the driveway.

                    MATT
          Are you sure? Because I had a lot of
          fun the last time.

With her back turned, Julie makes a face.

                    JULIE
               (to herself)
          Yeah, well...

She turns back.

                    JULIE (CONT'D)
          As I said, I'm busy--

She stops short. She sees Darren at the trash bin. Their eyes meet. Lightning bolts.

                    DARREN
          Hi.

                    JULIE
          Hi.

They stand there, transfixed. Matt is oblivious.

                    MATT
               (from the truck)
          Julie, that's Darren. Darren, that's
          Julie.

                    DARREN
          Nice to meet you.

Darren holds out his hand to shake. He's wearing big garbage man gloves covered with crud. Julie reacts.

                    DARREN (CONT'D)
          Sorry.

He takes off the glove and they shake hands.

                    JULIE
          So you're new on the "force."

                    DARREN
          Just trying to raise some dough to
          finish up college.

                    JULIE
          College. Cool. I'm applying now.

                    DARREN
          Where?

Matt HONKS THE HORN.

                    MATT
          Move it, molasses!

                    DARREN
               (to Julie)
          Gotta sprint.
               (heads to the truck)
          Hey, why don't you come play pool
          with us tonight?

Julie looks hopeful, but before she can say "yes"...

                    MATT
          She can't. She's "busy."

INT. MCKENNA KITCHEN - A LITTLE LATER

Gretchen is cleaning up, making sure the kitchen is spotless. There's still a place setting on the table. Evan comes in with his briefcase.

                    EVAN
          I'm off to work.

                    GRETCHEN
          Bye, sweetheart.

They kiss. Evan notices the empty place setting.

                    EVAN
          Corey didn't eat breakfast. Doesn't
          he have school?

                         GRETCHEN
          He says he doesn't feel well enough
          to go.

                         EVAN
          Bet he's well enough to play "Teenage
          Super Destroyer Whatever."

                         GRETCHEN
          You're the one who bought him his
          first computer when he was only three
          years old.

                         EVAN
          I thought it would help develop math
          aptitude and hand-eye coordination. I
          didn't know he'd end up with the
          social skills of a mole.

INT. COREY'S ROOM

Corey, a pale, 13-year-old, is at his computer playing a
game which involves a big guy and a little guy tied to
circular saws in a lumber mill. Corey manipulates the
controller with one hand and eats cold pizza from a box
by his side. Candy wrappers and soda cans are everywhere.
The room is dark. There is one small window that is
covered with a thick shade and lined with tin foil.

SFX: KNOCK ON THE DOOR

                         GRETCHEN (O.S.)
          Corey. Open up.

                         COREY
               (still playing)
          I'm sick.

                         GRETCHEN (O.S.)
          What's wrong?

                         COREY
               (swallows some pizza)
          My stomach hurts.

                         GRETCHEN (O.S.)
          It does not. You are faking, young
          man, and we both know it. You've had
          plenty of warning. I'm coming in.

Corey panics, throwing the pizza box under the computer
table as Gretchen opens up the door.

                         GRETCHEN (CONT'D)
          Now, listen--
               (wrinkling her nose)
                         (MORE)

                    GRETCHEN (CONT'D)
          Ohmigod, it smells like vomit in
          here. Corey, did you vomit?

                    COREY
          No.
                    (realizing)
          I mean, yeah. I vomited all over the
          place. I told you I was sick. That's
          why I can't go to school.

                    GRETCHEN
          And I thought you were faking. I'm
          sorry, Corey. Of course, you can stay
          home from school.

                    COREY
          Thanks, mom.

He fakes a gag.

                    GRETCHEN
          But you can't stay in your room all
          day. You need some fresh air.

Gretchen goes to the window lined with tin foil and PULLS
UP THE TINY SHADE. Sunlight streams in. Corey BLINKS.

                    COREY
                    (re: sunlight)
          Geez, Mom, you're glaring up my
          screen.

She opens the window.

                    GRETCHEN
          Much better. Now do you feel well
          enough to stay home alone or do you
          want me to call the law firm and tell
          them I'm not coming in?

                    COREY
                    (laying it on thick)
          That's a tough one, Mom.
                    (then)
          I think I'll just stay home alone.

                    GRETCHEN
          Okay, honey. Call if you need me. And
          if you feel better later, would you
          mind picking up around here? There's
          garbage everywhere.

EXT. COMMERCIAL STREET - MID MORNING

Darren is sitting in the garbage truck listening to his
smart phone through headphones. Matt is at the curb
moving bins around.

A nearby billboard reads: "PLASTECH THANKS NEWFIELD FOR TRYING (AND LOVING) CLEAN BAGS"

Matt notices one stray Clean bag that fell out of the bin. It's sitting on the curb in DIRECT SUNLIGHT.

FX: THE SUN PENETRATES THE BAG

Matt moves to pick it up. The bag appears to MOVE AWAY FROM HIM. He goes to pick it up again. It moves away from him again. Matt is perplexed. He looks back.

                    MATT
               (calling to Darren)
          Hey, did you see that?

Darren is listening to his music too loudly to notice. Matt makes another move toward the bag. This time, the bag disappears into an alley. Matt follows it.

                    MATT (V.O.)
          Weird. What's doing that?
               (gets it)
          Here, kitty, kitty. Did someone lock
          you in a Clean bag?

Matt disappears into the alley.

                    MATT (O.S.)
               (calling out)
          Come here, kitty, I want to help.
          I'm a friend--
               (suddenly scared)
          Hey, what's going on?
               (then)
          Ohmigod, get off me!!

SFX: MATT'S MUFFLED SCREAM AND PLASTIC RUSTLING

EXT. GARBAGE TRUCK - A FEW MINUTES LATER

Darren is still into his music. He looks in the rear view mirror. No sign of Matt.

SFX: HE HONKS THE HORN

Still no sign. In the rear view mirror, he sees...

AN EMPTY SOUP CAN ROLLS OUT OF THE ALLEY

Odd. Darren gets out of the truck to investigate.

                    DARREN
          Hey, Matt. Matt...

Darren picks up the can and heads to where it came from. He disappears down the alley.

                              DARREN (O.S.) (CONT'D)
          What the hell?!

EXT. ALLEY - DAY

Matt is lying in a pool of oozing garbage. A busted Clean
bag covers Matt's face. Darren tries to remove the bag,
but it's really shoved in there hard. Darren yanks and
the bag makes a SUCKING NOISE. The force of the pulls
knocks Darren back. He holds the busted bag in his hands
and goes back to look at his friend. Matt's face is a
bluish color.

                              DARREN
               Help! I need help!

INT. PLASTECH - EVAN'S OFFICE - DAY

Evan McKenna is in his sleek office at Plastech looking
at an advertisement for Clean bags along with GARY, in
his 20s, who is coordinating the Clean Green Festival.
The billboards picture a beautiful park with the sun
shining on a gleaming pile of Clean bags. The caption
reads: "CLEAN BAGS ARE COMING!! (P.S. They're
Biodegradable!)"

In the background is a DURABILITY TESTING MACHINE,
featuring a blunt wooden peg poking a bag full of
garbage. A tally on top keeps count of how many times the
bag has been poked. It reads 1,089,583.

                         EVAN
                    (re: the billboard)
               It's perfect, Gary. It's a terrific
               campaign.

                         GARY
               Thanks. It's all coming together.

CAROLINE, an attractive twenty-something woman, enters.
She's co-ordinating Clean bag's test marketing.

                         EVAN
               Caroline, come look at these
               billboard mock-ups. Gary outdid
               himself.

                         CAROLINE
               And you'll both want to see these.

Caroline hands them each a piece of paper.

                         GARY
                    (re: paper)
               I see numbers. Lots of numbers. You
               know I'm a visual person.

                         CAROLINE
         Then picture a roof with something
         going through it--because these are
         the results of the final survey from
         our local test marketing, and people
         are loving the Clean bag.

                          EVAN
         Wow. A ninety-eight percent approval
         rating.

                          GARY
         Hallelujah. I get the feeling there's
         going to be something special in our
         Christmas envelopes this year.

                         CAROLINE
                    (a little peeved)
         This is bigger than that, Gary. It
         isn't about bonuses. It's about
         making the world a better place.

                          EVAN
                    (stepping in)
         It's about both. We can do good and
         do well. Now, is everything set for
         the Green Festival, Gary?

                          GARY
         Yes, and it's going to be
         magnificent. We commissioned a
         sculpture by international art
         superstar Claes Oldenberg that will
         have everyone talking. A twenty-foot
         tall Clean bag. The image will
         dominate Pinterest and also appear on
         the cover of next month's Artforum.

                          EVAN
         I don't think that will sell more
         bags.

                          GARY
         No, but this will.
                    (whistles loudly)
         Meet the Bag-ettes!

MUSIC UP:

A door opens and THREE DANCING GARBAGE BAGS WITH KILLER
LEGS COME TAPPING in. The bags are tied above their heads
and cover their faces. As the bags form a kick line:

                      GARY (CONT'D)
         Aren't they gorgeous?

                    EVAN
                (to Caroline)
        He didn't even have the courtesy to
        let us see the women's faces.

                    CAROLINE
        Who says they're women?

The dance routine ends. Gary APPLAUDS.

                    GARY
                (to dancing bags)
        Fabulous. Except you on the right, we
        need more enthusiasm. You're a Clean
        bag. Act like it.

The bag on the right hangs its head as they file out.

                    GARY (CONT'D)
                (to Evan)
        Trust me, that enthusiasm problem
        will be cleared up by tomorrow.
        Everything will go as smooth as silk.

Evan smiles.

INT. POLICE STATION - DAY

Darren is being interrogated by OFFICER FOLEY. Officer
Foley is pointing to a blackboard which has a drawing of
the alley that Matt was hurt in.

                    OFFICER FOLEY
        I just don't get it. It's a dead-end
        alley. This is the only exit. And
        you're sure the truck was here?

                    DARREN
        Right where it's drawn.

                    OFFICER FOLEY
        And where were you?

                    DARREN
        I told you. In the truck.

                    OFFICER FOLEY
        So anyone running out of the alley,
        you would have seen?

                    DARREN
        Correct.

                    OFFICER FOLEY
        So what do you think happened to your
        friend?

                    DARREN
          I don't know. Maybe Matt tripped
          while carrying a bag and it hit his
          head.

                    OFFICER FOLEY
          Then how come the surgeon found this
          lodged in his trachea?

Office Foley holds up a plastic evidence bag which holds
a crushed yogurt container.

                    DARREN
          A yogurt container?

                    OFFICER FOLEY
          And you have no idea how your friend
          inhaled a garbage bag?

                    DARREN
          None. What does he say?

                    OFFICER FOLEY
          He's under heavy sedation and can't
          answer any questions.

                    DARREN
          Have you tested for fingerprints?

                    OFFICER FOLEY
              (slaps forehead)
          Fingerprints. I knew we forgot
          something!
              (then)
          Yes, we checked for fingerprints.
          Came up with nothing. No prints. No
          hair. No blood. Cleanest crime I've
          ever seen. All right, I'm done with
          you.
              (Darren starts out)
          Don't leave town. And hey, you might
          want to buy a lottery ticket.

                    DARREN
          Why?

                    OFFICER FOLEY
          You're on a lucky streak. It could
          have been you in the hospital now.

INT. BURGERMEISTER'S - DAY

A fast-food restaurant filled with the after-school
crowd. Julie works behind the counter. She hands an order
to a customer as DARREN ENTERS and gets in line.

                    JULIE
              (to customer)
        Would you like fries with that?

                    HUNGRY KID
        All I got was fries.

                    JULIE
        I know, but we have to ask.

The customer moves off. Darren is now at the front of the
line. Julie is marking something on her pad.

                    DARREN
              (looking at the
               posted menu)
        I'll have the--
              (looks down)
        Hey, it's you.

Julie looks up. She smiles. A pleasant surprise.

                    JULIE
        Well, hi.

                    DARREN
        I didn't know you worked here.

                    JULIE
        Yeah. Just trying to keep you garbage
        guys in business.
              (she smiles)
        So what'll you have?

                    DARREN
        I'll have a --

As Darren looks up at the posted menu, TWO BULLIES
approach and start to roast him.

                    BULLY #1
        Look who's here.
              (sniffs)
        Guess Burgermeister's doesn't have a
        "No shower--no service" policy.

                    DARREN
              (ignoring him; to
               Julie)
        I'll have a Bacon Meister and fries,
        please.

Julie punches the order in.

                         BULLY #2
          You know, I'm surprised you can even
          eat after what happened to your
          buddy.

                         BULLY #1
          Yeah, we hear Matt got <u>trashed</u> this
          morning.

The bullies CRACK UP.

                         DARREN
          It's not funny.

                         BULLY #1
          Sure it is. Instead of him taking out
          the garbage... the garbage took out
          him!

The bullies LAUGH some more. Darren grabs one of them
roughly.

                         DARREN
          That's enough! Matt's hurt and unless
          either of you want to join him, I
          suggest you go somewhere else for
          your greasy burgers.

Darren shoves him aside. The bullies move off, scared.

                         DARREN (CONT'D)
          Idiots. They just don't get it.

                         JULIE
          I know how you feel, Darren. Matt is
          kind of a creep, but he doesn't
          deserve that.

                         DARREN
          No one deserves that.

                         JULIE
          I was just thinking, if you're upset
          and want someone to talk to, maybe I
          could be that person.

                         DARREN
          You mean it?

                         JULIE
          Yeah, sure.

                         DARREN
          How about we talk tonight?

                         JULIE
          Tonight?
                    (smiles)
          Okay. I get off at seven. You
          remember where my house is? I'll
          sneak out around ten.

                         DARREN
          I'll see you then.

He starts to go.

                         JULIE
          Hey, Darren. You forgot your "greasy
          burgers."

She hands him the bag, then hands onto it for one more
second to hold him back.

                         JULIE (CONT'D)
          One more question--

                         DARREN
          Who hurt Matt? I wish I knew.
          Probably some trash bum who's still
          out there.

                         JULIE
          Actually, I was just going to ask if
          you want fries with that.

As they share a sheepish look...

EXT. ALLEY BEHIND BURGERMEISTER - DAY

The BULLIES are walking behind the restaurant where
there's a LARGE DUMPSTER FILLED WITH CLEAN BAGS.
Burgermeister food and packaging is all over the ground.
Sun streams into the alley. Bully #1 kicks some garbage.

                         BULLY #1
          I don't care what he says. Someone
          getting injured by a garbage bag is
          hilarious.

                         BULLY #2
          No arguments here.

BULLY #1 LIFTS THE TOP OF THE DUMPSTER, EXPOSING THE BAGS
TO SUNLIGHT, then he GRABS a Clean bag and throws it onto
the ground.

                         BULLY
                    (mockingly; to bag)
          Hey, you crusty old sack, come at me.
          Come at me.

The BAG FLIES in Bully #1's face, knocking him to the ground. Bully #2 looks on in disbelief as his friend struggles underneath the bag. His cut-off tee shows his MUSCLES RIPPLING to fight the bag, but it's no use. His CRIES ARE MUFFLED by the suffocation.

                         BULLY #2
              I'll go get help.

Bully #2 takes off. As he passes the dumpster, all the BAGS LEAP OUT AND PILE on top of him. For a few moments the bags SHAKE as Bully #2 struggles underneath.

EXT. BACKYARD - DAY

MRS. KLEIN, a middle-aged woman in a sun hat, is raking her backyard. As she fills a Clean bag with leaves:

                         MRS. KLEIN
              I've had enough of you leaves
              cluttering up my nice lawn. Why
              can't you fall in neat piles?

Mrs. Klein puts the last of the leaves in and tightly CLICKS the yellow Clickertop. She brings the bag over to a pile of five other Clean bags sitting IN THE SUN. She sets the bag down, then looks out her spotless lawn.

BEHIND HER BACK, the bags start to move toward her.

                         MRS. KLEIN (CONT'D)
              That's more like it.

THE BAGS MOVE CLOSER AND CLOSER.

                         MRS. KLEIN (CONT'D)
              Everything all tidy.

The bags jump Mrs. Klein from behind. She THRASHES around a little, but the old lady is no match for the bags. A single leaf floats through the air and lands on her hand.

EXT. THE STORM CELLAR DOORS OF A SCHOOL - DAY

A JANITOR is in the basement at the bottom of the stairs, tossing up Clean bags. There's a big pile at the top soaking up the sun. He throws the last bag out and GRUNTS. The janitor starts up the stairs.

                         JANITOR
              Why bother? They're just going to
              make more tomorrow.

The janitor is one step away from the top. He takes one more step and WHOOMP! A Clean bag knocks him down the steps.

19

As the bags roll down the steps...

INT. MR. LANCASTER'S OFFICE - SIX P.M.

MR. LANCASTER, President and CEO of Plastech, sits in his imposing chair, reviewing and signing letters. Everything in the office is strong, rich and leathery--including Lancaster.

Mr. Lancaster's SECRETARY ushers Evan in.

                    MR. LANCASTER
          McKenna, I wanted an update on
          Saturday's plans.

                    EVAN
          We're right on track. There will be
          something for everyone at the Clean
          Green Festival. And when it's over,
          we'll launch the trucks so all of
          America will experience the joys of
          Plastech Clean bags.

                    MR. LANCASTER
          You sound like one of your press
          releases. Look, we both know the
          product is a big improvement over
          last year's flawed model. Let's just
          hope the consumer feels the same. You
          can go now.

Mr. Lancaster goes back to his paperwork.

                    EVAN
          Thank you, sir.

Evan spots a photograph of a three-year-old boy on Mr. Lancaster's desk.

                    EVAN (CONT'D)
          There'll be a petting zoo if you want
          to bring your grandson to the Clean
          Green Festival.

                    MR. LANCASTER
               (looks up)
          My grandson?

                    EVAN
               (gestures to photo)
          Yes. Awfully cute.

                    MR. LANCASTER
          That's my son, McKenna. Not my
          grandson. My <u>son</u>. But perhaps you
          think both he and his mother would
          enjoy the petting zoo?

20

INT. MCKENNA HOUSE - DINING ROOM - NIGHT

Evan and Gretchen are setting the table for four.

                    GRETCHEN
          Oh, Evan, how could you?

                    EVAN
          I didn't know.

                    GRETCHEN
          So what did you say?

                    EVAN
          Nothing. I just left. Then I spent
          the next hour trying to think of what
          I could have said and the best I came
          up with was, "Nice shooting for a guy
          your age."

                    GRETCHEN
          Maybe it's better that you left.
               (calling out)
          Kids! Dinner!
               (to Evan)
          Wash your hands.

As he goes to the sink and washes his hands.

                    EVAN
          It was the last thing I needed today.
          My job is so on the line.

Julie enters. She walks over to the counter.

                    JULIE
               (lifting up the lid
                of the crock pot)
          What's for dinner?

                    GRETCHEN
          Spotted owl. Sit down. Where's your
          brother?

                    JULIE
          Gee, I wonder.

INT. COREY'S ROOM - NIGHT

Corey is still playing computer games. He holds a soda
can in his left hand and works the joystick with his
right.

SFX: A KNOCK

                    EVAN (O.S.)
          Corey, did you hear your mother?

                    COREY
          I'm busy.

                    EVAN (O.S.)
          It's dinnertime.

                    COREY
          Not hungry.

Evan bursts in. He's angry.

                    EVAN
          I've had enough of these games. You
          are going to have human contact
          tonight, young man.

Evan takes the joystick away.

                    COREY
          No!

                    EVAN
          Even if it kills you.

SFX: COREY'S VIDEO SCREEN CHARACTER IS BLOWN INTO A
MILLION PIECES.

                    COREY
             Literally.

INT. DINING ROOM - A LITTLE LATER

The family eats in silence. Finally:

                    COREY
          Oh, yeah, this is much more fun.

                    EVAN
          I'm sure someone has an amusing story
          to tell.

                    JULIE
          I heard two more people were found
          smothered by Clean bags. One was an
          old lady who was out gardening and
          the other was a janitor at the middle
          school.

                    EVAN
          What's amusing about that?

                    JULIE
          Well, when they found the janitor,
          they thought his brains had spilled
          out but it turned out to be just
          lasagna from the cafeteria. Isn't
          that gross?

                         GRETCHEN
          Yes. And it's hardly dinner table
          conversation.

                         COREY
          Garbage bags that take out humans
          would make an awesome game. Man vs.
          junk in an epic battle for the
          survival of planet Earth--

                         EVAN
                    (jumping in)
          Enough of that talk! Clean bags are
          the future for both this country and
          this family and if you don't have
          something nice to say about them,
          shut up and eat.

Silence. Dead silence. Julie eyes a sealed Clean bag in
the corner suspiciously. Just then, the TRASH SETTLES and
the bag SHIFTS. Julie JUMPS, startled.

INT. COREY'S ROOM - NIGHT

Corey rushes into his room and shuts the door behind him
quickly. He stands next to the door.

                         COREY
                    (a vow)
          Human interaction. That will never
          happen again.

Corey sits down at the COMPUTER AND FLIPS IT ON. As it
boots, he grabs a Jolt soda in his left hand. Corey
clicks on the "start" button. It starts at ZERO. Corey
starts to play.

INT. COREY'S ROOM - TEN O'CLOCK

The score stands at over 50,000.

INT. JULIE'S ROOM - TEN O'CLOCK

It's ten o'clock. Julie is dressed and halfway out the
window. There's a KNOCK on the door. Julie freezes.

                         GRETCHEN (O.S.)
               'Night, Julie. Don't study too late.

                         JULIE
          I won't, Mom. Promise.

Julie climbs out the window.

23.

EXT. MCKENNA HOUSE - NIGHT

Julie drops onto the roof of the garage. She tip-toes
across the roof and deftly shimmies down the drainpipe.
She runs down the driveway to a PARKED BEAT UP SAAB WITH
THE LIGHTS OUT. It's a dark night. She can't see into the
car. As she opens the door:

                    JULIE
          Hey--

The CAR LIGHT GOES ON, revealing a GARBAGE BAG SITTING IN
THE FRONT SEAT. IT TURNS TOWARD JULIE.

                    JULIE (CONT'D)
          Aaahhhhh!

The bag starts to LAUGH.

                    BAG (V.O.)
          Easy, Julie, it's just me.

Darren lifts the bag up over his head. He's pleased his
joke worked so well.

                    DARREN
          See, I just put a bag over my head--

                    JULIE
          Which is incredibly stupid. You could
          suffocate!

                    DARREN
              (off her expression)
          You're right. It was stupid. Very
          stupid. Stupider than the stupidest
          thing any stupid person has ever
          stupidly done.

Julie looks at him. He is awfully cute. She gets in and
shuts the door.

                    JULIE
          Drive.

EXT. BONE HILL (ATOP PLASTECH PARK) - NIGHT

Darren's Saab pulls up a steep road and gets to the top
where there's a flat area overlooking the city.

Down the sloping hill is a park. The car windows are
open. Darren pulls into the flat area and stops the car.

                    DARREN
          So was this a pet cemetery? Is that
          why they call it "Bone Hill?"

                    JULIE
Uh, it's not really called "Bone
Hill." That's just something the kids
call it because, you know, they
sometimes--

                    DARREN
Oh. Right. Got it.
          (then)
Well, it's pretty up here, isn't it?
I know God was in a hurry when he
built this stuff but he's really good
at his job.

                    JULIE
It's a landfill. It's all man-made.
When I was a kid this entire area was
flat. They even trucked the trees in.

                    DARREN
Wow.

                    JULIE
Actually, it used to be this farm. It
was owned by a beekeeper named
"Albie." He had about twenty hives
and all the kids used to bike over
and, for a quarter, he'd give you a
chunk of honeycomb. It was so
delicious. The beeswax had a feel all
its own, neither hard nor soft. And
you'd take it into your mouth and
work it over with your tongue. And
pretty soon you'd feel the hot honey
pouring down your throat. It was
amazing.

                    DARREN
          (voice cracking)
Really?

He shifts in his seat.

                    JULIE
But then about ten years ago,
Plastech offered Albie a lot of money
for the land. They said they were
going to build a park so he agreed.
But what Plastech didn't tell him was
that first, they were going to fill
it with garbage. People in the town
were angry at Albie. They thought it
was all his fault. I mean everyone
makes garbage, but no on wants a
landfill in their backyard.

                    DARREN
So what happened to Albie?

                    JULIE
I don't know. I think he moved away.
He should have stuck around. The park
turned out nice and I think people
would have forgiven him.

                    DARREN
That's a nice story. I love to hear
you talk.

                    JULIE
You do?

                    DARREN
Yeah. I like to watch your mouth
move. You have a beautiful mouth.
        (moving in)
It's really expressive and warm--

                    JULIE
That's so nice of you to say, Darren.
So many men focus on other parts of
the body, but I think the mouth--

Darren puts his hand up.

                    DARREN
I know it can talk. Let's see what
else it can do.

He leans forward for a kiss.

INT. MCKENNA MASTER BEDROOM - NIGHT

Gretchen and Evan are in bed. He stares into space as she
tries to read.

                    EVAN
It's the Hefty people. I know it.

                    GRETCHEN
What?

                    EVAN
They're trying to ruin the launch of
the Clean bag.

                    GRETCHEN
So they hired someone to try to
smother an old lady, a janitor and
assorted others?

                         EVAN
          They're ruthless. Who knows what
          they'll do to keep their market
          share.

                         GRETCHEN
          You're insane. I can't believe anyone
          would be happy about those tragedies.

                         EVAN
          That's why you're not in marketing.

                         GRETCHEN
          Then maybe you should get out of it.
          If that's the kind of people who are
          doing it.

                         EVAN
                 (defensive)
          You know exactly why I'm doing it.

Evan takes the tissue box from the nightstand and starts
pulling a tissue out for each reason he gives.

                         EVAN (CONT'D)
          So we can live in this nice house.
                 (pulls a tissue)
          So Julie can go to college.
                 (pulls a tissue)
          So Corey can have a backyard he never
          plays in.
                 (pulls a tissue)
          So we can waste tissues.

Gretchen gets up and moves toward the door.

                         GRETCHEN
          Well, maybe it's time we stop
          sacrificing our principles to pay the
          mortgage. Maybe it's not worth it to
          live this well.

She exits. Evan balls up the tissues and throws them in
the trash.

EXT. BONE HILL - NIGHT

Julie and Darren are still making out.

SFX: A DOG WHIMPERS

Julie pulls back.

SFX: A DOG WHIMPERS

                         JULIE
          Did you hear that?

                    DARREN
          What?

                    JULIE
          I think it's a dog crying.

SFX: A DOG WHIMPERS

                    JULIE (CONT'D)
          Poor puppy.

                    DARREN
               (dismissive)
          He's fine.

Darren moves to make out more. Julie is more concerned
about the dog.

                    JULIE
          But it sounds like he's hurt.

                    DARREN
          You're using your tongue to make
          words again.

                    JULIE
          You don't know me very well if you
          think I can just ignore an animal's
          pain.
               (opens car door)
          You can make out without me.

Darren stops her.

                    DARREN
          No. You stay here.
               (begrudging)
          I'll go see if the dog's okay.

                    JULIE
               (smiles)
          Thanks.

Darren gets out as Julie settles back into the car with
the door open, which sheds a SMALL AMOUNT OF LIGHT.

                                        INTERCUT WITH:

EXT. GROUNDS - NIGHT

Darren passes some low shrubs and a stand with a
historical marker next to a row of rest area-type metal
garbage bins. Down below is the landfill area marked by:

THREE LONG PIPES WITH GAS FLAMES AT THE TOP

SFX: A DOG WHIMPERS

                         JULIE (CONT'D)
                    (calls out; points)
              It's coming from over there.

Darren moves into a dark and shadowy area.

SFX: A RUSTLE IN THE BUSHES

                         DARREN
              Something's in the bushes.

He heads over to the bushes. Julie starts to get nervous.

                         JULIE
              Be careful, Darren.

                         DARREN
              Don't worry. It's only a little dog.

Darren squeezes behind the metal garbage bins and
finds...

A SMALL WHIMPERING DOG.

Darren approaches.

                         DARREN (CONT'D)
              Hi, boy. Are you lost? Don't be
              scared.

As Darren leans over to pick up the dog, A WILD-EYED BUM
LEAPS OUT OF THE CLOSEST GARBAGE CAN.

                         BUM
              Aaaaaaaahhh!!

Darren jumps back in fright and starts to lose his
balance. The bum shoves Darren to the ground. The bum
CLAMBERS OUT OF THE CAN and grabs the dog protectively.

                         BUM (CONT'D)
                    (a prophecy)
              They're coming! They're coming!

THE BUM RUSHES THE CAR. He has garbage tied around his
waist. Julie quickly CLOSES THE DOOR AND LOCKS THEM.

She presses the switch to ROLL UP HER WINDOW, but they're
POWER WINDOWS and won't work with the engine off. As she
fumbles to turn on the ignition.

                         JULIE
              Darren!

Darren stands up. He grabs a rock. The bum is fast
approaching the car. Over Julie's SCREAMS:

                         BUM
          There's no escape. They're coming!

Julie gets the POWER ON and starts rolling up the window,
but the bum sticks his hand in. Julie SCREAMS as the
bum's face is right up against the glass.

Darren appears behind the bum and raises the rock. He's
about to bring it down, when Julie gets a look over her
face.

                        JULIE
          No, wait! Don't hit him!

                       DARREN
                 (stops himself)
          Huh?

                        JULIE
          It's Albie! The honey guy. Don't hurt
          him! Albie, it's Julie McKenna.

Albie looks at her, calming down at the sound of his
name. Julie rolls down the window.

                    JULIE (CONT'D)
          I used to play here. At your farm.
          Before the landfill.

Albie reacts strongly to her last word. He looks around
as if he were surrounded and under attack.

                       DARREN
          We're no going to hurt you.

Julie gets out of the car.

                        JULIE
          Albie, you don't look so good. Is
          everything okay?

                       ALBIE
          They're coming! They're coming!

                        JULIE
          Who's coming?

                       ALBIE
          The sins of the past will be visited
          upon the land. Listen and I'll tell
          you.

Albie walks over to the tin garbage drums. He picks up
two sticks and starts to POUND OUT A TRIBAL RHYTHM ON THE
GARBAGE DRUMS.

                              ALBIE (CONT'D)
                         (to the rhythm)
          I leaned over by a tree/ And here's
          what the trash can said to me/ "Our
          numbers are growing, it's nearing
          time for our birth/ For when all the
          landfills are full, garbage will walk
          the EARTH!

Albie finishes with a LOUD CRESCENDO THEN KICKS THE CAN
DOWN THE HILLSIDE. GARBAGE BAGS SPILL OUT AND ROLL DOWN
THE HILL, SPREADING ACROSS THE COUNTRYSIDE.

EXT. STREET ALONGSIDE PLASTECH PARK -- THE NEXT MORNING

SFX: A CAR HORN BLASTS

Traffic is stopped. A traffic worker in an orange neon
vest holds up a stop sign as a repair truck blocks the
street.

Evan is first in the line of cars. He HONKS impatiently.

                              EVAN
                         (out his car window)
          Come on!

                              TRAFFIC WORKER
          Relax, sir. We'll have you moving in
          a moment.

                              EVAN
                         (to himself)
          Right. Relax. What do I have to be
          uptight about?

Evan looks over at a sign strung up at the park's
entrance that reads: "PLASTECH PRESENT THE FIRST ANNUAL
CLEAN GREEN FESTIVAL SATURDAY MUSIC-PRIZES-GAMES-ANIMALS-
ART."

                              EVAN (CONT'D)
          What's going on anyway?

                              TRAFFIC WORKER
          There's a problem with the landfill's
          gas recovery system so they're
          sending in some machinery to re-open
          the pipe.

Workers are digging around the area of the THREE POLES
WITH GAS FLAMES. Only TWO of the three are now lit. The
other is out.

                              EVAN
          You're kidding. How long's that going
          to take?

                    TRAFFIC WORKER
          Should be done by the time the
          festival starts tomorrow.

                         EVAN
          "Should?" "Should?"
                    (something drops on
                     his windshield)
          Was that a drop of rain?

EXT. ALLEY BEHIND BURGERMEISTER'S - DAY

It's overcast except for one cloud break just over the
alley.

A garbage truck driven by Darren pulls up alongside the
alley. DARREN HOPS OUT. He's working solo. He leaves the
TRUCK RUNNING and sprints into the alley. He picks up two
bags in each hand and starts for the truck when he sees
something peeking out from under another bag. He nudges
the bag with his foot and out POPS A HUMAN HAND!

Darren starts breathing heavily and quickly removes more
bags. He is shocked to discover the TWO DEAD BULLIES. He
looks around the alley. No one else appears to be around.
A SHAFT OF LIGHT hits a stray bag. It starts to wiggle.
Darren notices it. He moves towards it a few inches.

The bag moves toward him a few inches. Darren moves
forward another few inches. The bag moves forward another
few inches. Darren starts to move forward, then turns and
BOLTS FOR THE TRUCK.

The bag ROLLS AFTER HIM. Darren is running as fast as he
can. He makes it to the truck. Just as Darren opens the
door, the BAG LAUNCHES ITSELF at his back, knocking him
down. Darren struggles to his feet.

He WRESTLES with the bag and manages to fling it away.
The bag FLINGS itself back at his head, but Darren ducks
just in time and the bag goes flying. It lands on the
ground and quickly turns and heads back, but Darren jumps
into the truck and closes the door. Darren puts the truck
in gear and starts to move. He picks up speed and is
getting away until...

The BAG FLINGS ITSELF ON THE WINDSHIELD. Darren is
startled and the truck SWERVES. He tries to see but the
bag is blocking his view. The truck bounces off the curb.

Darren is determined to knock the bag off. He turns on
the windshield wipers. They break off. He turns the truck
hard to the left, then hard to the right. Then hard to
the left, and hard to the right. The force knocks the bag
a little off-center, allowing Darren to see out the
windshield. He sees:

32

A TREE DIRECTLY IN HIS PATH

Darren SLAMS on the brakes. Too late. The TRUCK CRASHES INTO THE TREE. The force causes the BAG TO FLY INTO THE AIR. Darren falls forward over the steering wheel.

SFX: MECHANICAL CRUNCHING NOISES

Then all is quiet. Darren is more dazed than hurt. He rubs his neck and looks out the front window. He can't see the rogue bag. He looks out the sides. Still, no bag. With trepidation, he opens the door. He gets out.

THE SKY IS OVERCAST. He stands under the tree to assess the damage of the truck. Just then:

Something THICK AND RED drops on his shoulder. It looks like blood. Darren stiffens. More red stuff drips. It dawns on Darren. He touches the red stuff and sniffs it.

                    DARREN
          Ketchup.

Darren laughs then looks directly overhead and sees:

THE BAG HANGING ON A BRANCH

The bag has been PIERCED THROUGH THE MIDDLE. Burgermeister garbage is falling through the tear.

SFX: TEARING NOISE

                    DARREN (CONT'D)
          Oh no.

Darren quickly dives out from under the bag which cascades to the ground. Cartons, dirty napkins, cups and half-eaten food tumble out. The bag falls, too.

Darren moves carefully to examine the bag. He nudges it with his foot. He looks at the outside and doesn't see anything unusual. He turns what's left of it inside out. He sees a marking on the material. He peers closely and sees THE PLASTECH LOGO:

EXT. PLASTECH BUILDING - DAY

The same logo is on the building.

INT. MCKENNA'S OFFICE - DAY

Caroline and Gary are waiting when Evan rushes in.

                    EVAN
          Sorry. I hit bad traffic. They're
          building a trench in the landfill
          and--

33

He sees Caroline and Gary's faces. They look devastated.

                    EVAN (CONT'D)
          Why are you looking like that? What
          happened? Did somebody die?

                    CAROLINE
          Worse.

She steps away revealing that the DURABILITY TESTING
MACHINE has stopped. The bag is pierced by the dull
wooden peg. The final tally count reads 2,110,666.

                    CAROLINE (CONT'D)
          Isn't it awful?

                    EVAN
          It was bound to happen some time.

                    GARY
          But not so soon. We already sent out
          literature saying the bag could stand
          up to three million pokes.

                    EVAN
          Let's not forget we're still two
          times stronger than all the other
          leading brands.

                    CAROLINE
               (snapping)
          But we're not as strong as we
          thought!

                    EVAN
          I don't see why you're so upset.

                    CAROLINE
               (blurting it out)
          I just think the bags should have
          been tested more before the launch,
          that's all.

There's silence as that sinks in. Evan's SECRETARY
enters.

                    SECRETARY
          Mr. McKenna, there's a Darren Higgins
          here to see you. He says it's an
          emergency.

                    EVAN
          I don't have time--

Darren pushes his way in. One arm is behind his back.

                    DARREN
          This bag tried to kill me.

Darren throws the ripped bag to the ground.

                    DARREN (CONT'D)
          I know it sounds strange, but your
          Clean bags are alive. And they're
          attacking people. You've got to do
          something.

Caroline, Gary and Evan all exchange looks. Then Evan
BREAKS INTO APPLAUSE.

                    EVAN
          Very impressive. A riveting
          performance. Now go tell your bosses
          at Hefty that you succeeded in
          wasting our time.

                    DARREN
          I don't work for Hefty. I'm a garbage
          man and, yesterday, I found my friend
          Matt, almost smothered, by a bag of
          garbage. Today, I discovered two more
          dead.

                    GARY
          And you're assuming it's the bags and
          not some maniac with a bag?

                    DARREN
          I saw it with my own eyes. A bag
          attacked me. I ran as fast as I
          could, but the bag followed. I jumped
          into my truck and it jumped onto my
          windshield. It was trying to make me
          crash. Finally, I slammed into a tree
          which sent the bag flying and a
          branch pierced it. Only then did it
          stop.

                    GARY
          Like a wooden stake through its
          heart...

                    DARREN
          Exactly.
               (realizing)
          Now you're just trying to make it
          sound stupid or supernatural. Look, I
          know what I saw. These are new
          experimental bags, right?

                         EVAN
          They're hardly "experimental."
          They've been tested in the lab and
          the community. There are already
          thousands in the landfill. I use them
          in my own home with my own family.

Evan gestures to a photo of his family on the desk.
Darren REACTS when he sees the photo of Julie.

                         DARREN
          But there's something you didn't
          figure on. Something that's causing
          them to do this. What did you use to
          make these bags, anyway?

                         EVAN
          We're busy people, Darren. We don't
          have time for this.

                         DARREN
          I want to know.

                         EVAN
                (shows him the door)
          If you'll excuse us--

Darren refuses to budge.

                         DARREN
          And if you don't tell me, I'll stand
          at the entrance of the Clean Green
          Festival tomorrow shouting to the
          press that Clean bags are toxic. Is
          that what you want?

Evan realizes that he's over the barrel.

INT. LAB AT PLASTECH - DAY

The lab is an airy, spotlessly white room. DR. LINDA
HARTKE is hunched over an experiment, her face is hidden
when Evan and Darren walk in.

                         EVAN
          This is the lab where the Clean Bag
          was developed. The R&D team was
          headed by Dr. Hartke.
                (sees Dr. Hartke)
          Ah, there you are.

                         DARREN
          Hi. I'm Darren.

                         EVAN
          He thinks the bags you made have come
          alive.

                         DR. HARTKE
          Really?

Dr. Hartke, a lovely, young British scientist, turns and
stands.

                         DARREN
          I know it sounds stupid, Dr. Hartke-

                         DR. HARTKE
          Call me "Dr. Frankenstein."

                         DARREN
          If you could maybe answer my
          questions--

                         EVAN
          You received your Ph.D. In molecular
          biology from Oxford, right, Dr.
          Hartke?

                         DR. HARTKE
          Correct.

                         EVAN
               (condescending; to
                Darren)
          I think she'll be able to answer your
          questions.

                         DARREN
          I just want to know what these bags
          are made out of.

                         DR. HARTKE
          The usual. High-quality number three
          polyethylene, which as you know, is a
          simple polmerized ethylene resin --
          and ten percent state-required PCR.

                         DARREN
          Which is?

                         DR. HARTKE
          Post Consumer Resin, better known as
          recycled detergent bottles.

                         DARREN
          That's all?

                         DR. HARTKE
          Not quite. There's also the not so
          usual.

                         DARREN
          Which is...

                    DR. HARTKE
          ...what makes our bags uniquely
          biodegradable and a trade secret. But
          I assure you every one of the
          products is all-natural. Common
          substances made by Mother Nature.

                    DARREN
          I need to know what they are.

                    DR. HARTKE
          I can't tell you. Except to say every
          one of the products is all-natural
          and come to you thanks to the
          goodness of Mother Nature.

                    DARREN
              (losing patience)
          Oh, come on. I think these bags are
          somehow alive and you won't tell me
          what's causing it?

                    DR. HARTKE
          If you can prove to me that these
          bags are somehow "animating," I'll be
          concerned. Until then, good day.

                    DARREN
          Fine. I'll show you. All I need is a
          full bag of garbage.

Darren grabs a Clean bag from the shelf and starts
filling it, emptying a trash can into it. He stops at the
coffee station and dumps paper cups, sugar packets,
stirrers, and napkins into the bag. He picks up the
coffee pot filled with steaming coffee and holds it over
the open bag.

                    DARREN (CONT'D)
          Can it take it?

                    DR. HARTKE
          Of course. I designed the Clean bag
          to withstand heat up to 300 degrees.
          It's a full millimeter thick so you
          could even add this--
              (she picks up a rock
               door stop)
          The bag can easily hold forty pounds.

Darren dumps the coffee in and, then, adds the rock.

                    DARREN
          Okay, this feels nice and full. Now I
          just have to close it...

38

Darren takes the yellow Clickertop off the side and
starts to close it.

                    DARREN (CONT'D)
          Wait. I'd better take this thing
          outdoors in case it goes nuts.
                    (pointing at the
                     sliding glass doors)
          Can I go out there?

                    DR. HARTKE
          Sure.

                    EVAN
                    (noticing)
          Dammit. It's still raining.

Darren slides open the door and goes onto the roof/patio.

                              INTERCUT WITH:

EXT. ROOF PATIO - DAY

Darren shuts the door behind. He is still visible from
the lab. He starts to tie the bag. Dr. Hartke and Evan
turn their backs and talk casually.

                    EVAN
          Are you coming to the festival
          tomorrow?

                    DR. HARTKE
          Yes. I'm bringing my niece and
          nephew.

Darren slides the door back open and sticks his head in.

                    DARREN
          If the bag goes for my throat, you
          will come rescue me, right?

          DR. HARTKE   EVAN
Absolutely.   Be there in a second.

Phony smiles. Darren shuts the door and goes back into
the rain. He gives the bag one more twist then sets it
down quickly and backs off.

Dr. Hartke and Evan watch Darren as you would watch a
circus freak show. The bag just sits there. Darren
approaches it with trepidation, prods it with his foot,
then jumps back.

Still nothing from the bag. Darren looks at Evan and Dr.
Hartke and mouths, "WATCH THIS." Darren picks up the bag
and throws it, expecting it to retaliate. The bag doesn't
budge.

39

Darren smack himself on the chest in the universal "come at me" gesture. That doesn't work either so Darren kicks the bag. Nothing. He moves back to take a running start, then heads toward the bag and SLIPS ON THE SLICKNESS. HE FALLS ON HIS BUTT HARD.

INT. MCKENNA'S LAUNDRY ROOM - LATE AFTERNOON

Darren is standing in the room when Julie enters, carrying two boxes of frozen vegetables.

> JULIE
> You have your choice: peas or vegetable medley.

> DARREN
> Medley.

Julie hands him the package. He slips it under his pants.

> JULIE
> That ought to keep the swelling down.

Darren smiles.

> DARREN
> When I saw that photo of you in that office, I almost lost it.

> JULIE
> My dad's been at Plastech for ten years now. I wish I had known you were going. I could have saved you the trip.

> DARREN
> Why?

> JULIE
> Because for some weird reason, I don't think my dad's involved in a scheme of programming garbage bags to kill people.

> DARREN
> I never said the bags were programmed to kill people. I just think people get killed when they get in their way.

> JULIE
> But didn't Dr. Hartke say that the bags were all-natural?

Darren pulls away, annoyed.

                    DARREN
          What does that mean? The box
          jellyfish has an "all-natural" venom
          that can kill a human being in under
          four minutes. What makes you think
          Nature is good? It isn't. Nature is
          just things struggling to survive.

Julie looks at him for a beat. Does she believe him?

                    JULIE
          So what do you want to do?

                    DARREN
          Dr. Hartke was hiding something from
          me. I need to get back into the lab.
          Can you get the key to your dad's
          office building?

                    JULIE
          I don't know. I mean if we get
          caught, I would be in big trouble.
          Definitely grounded.

                    DARREN
          People have already been permanently
          "grounded," Julie. Do you want there
          to be more?

                    JULIE
          No.

                    DARREN
          Then get the key.

Julie nods.

INT. COREY'S ROOM - NIGHT

Corey is playing the same game. He still holds a can of
soda in his left hand but now he is on his bed holding
the controls on his knees.

His score is up to: 1,289,780.

EXT. MCKENNA HOUSE -- NIGHT

Evan lets himself into the house, drops his briefcase in
the foyer and heads to the kitchen like a man possessed.

INT. KITCHEN -- NIGHT

Without breaking stride, Evan heads straight for the
refrigerator. He opens the door and stands there,
looking.

ANGLE ON THE REFRIGERATOR

The fridge is packed with pre-packaged foods--snack packs, etc... Evan opens the fruit bin and finds Fruit Roll-Ups inside. JULIE ENTERS.

                    EVAN
          Hey, Jules.

                    JULIE
          Hey, Dad. How was work today?

Evan pulls out a foot-long, thin sandwich snack pack marked "Mini Ham and Cheese Sandwich--individually wrapped for Fffffffreshness!" The box has compartments for each item. He brings it to the table. He PULLS A SWISS ARMY KNIFE OUT OF HIS POCKET and slits open the package. Evan starts assembling the sandwich.

                    EVAN
          Fine. The national launch I've been
          working on for the past year is
          tomorrow. But I'm fine.

Julie helps him unwrap each individually wrapped slice of ham (three pieces) and cheese (two pieces) and bread (two slices) and an individually wrapped slice of pickle. The slices are tiny--two inches by two inches.

                    EVAN (CONT'D)
          I mean the last person that launched
          a Plastech product was Ann Peaslee
          who was convinced the see-through bag
          would be the next big thing. But then
          no one wanted to see their garbage
          after they threw it away, so Plastech
          just threw Ann Peaslee away. And now
          that I think about it, I'm pretty
          tense.

Julie unwraps two slices of bread while Evan unwraps the mini-knife that comes with the kit and opens the packet of mustard which he starts spreading.

                    JULIE
          You know what I think would make you
          feel better? Taking off your coat and
          tie.

                    EVAN
               (tossing her a pickle
                in a packet)
          See if you can open this. I don't
          think Houdini could get at this
          pickle.

Evan takes off his coat and tie and throws it over the chair while Julie tears at the pickle package with her teeth. It opens.

                    JULIE
          Incisors.

Julie quickly finishes assembling the sandwich.

                    JULIE (CONT'D)
          Here you go.

Julie turns, holding a plate with the TINY SANDWICH.
Behind her is a HUGE MOUND OF TRASH created by the
packaging.

                    EVAN
          Looks kind of small. Wait, my beer.

Evan opens the refrigerator again as Julie sidles over to
his suit. As he searches for a drink, Julie SLIPS HER
HAND into his suit breast pocket and pulls out his
wallet. Evan starts to stand.

                    JULIE
               (quickly)
          Would you get me a V-8? They're way
          in the back.

Evan fishes around for a V-8 as Julie fishes around for
his KEYCARD.

                    EVAN
               (into fridge)
          But you know, Julie, what makes going
          through all this work crap
          worthwhile?

                    JULIE
          The pension plan?

Julie finds the keycard, removes it from the wallet and
closes the wallet back up.

                    EVAN
               (into fridge)
          Knowing I'm providing for my family.

Evan straightens up and looks at Julie just as she drops
the wallet back into the suit pocket. Julie palms the
keycard. Evan closes the refrigerator door.

                    EVAN (CONT'D)
          Your mother, your brother, and you
          are all that matters to me in the
          world. I mean that, Julie.
               (he hugs her)
          You're what's honest and solid and
          good.

As Evan hugs Julie, she hides the keycard in her hand behind his back and silently dies.

EXT. CAR - NIGHT

Darren is in the front seat. Julie opens the door.

                    DARREN
      Did you get it?

Julie holds up the keycard.

                    JULIE
      Sorry it took so long, but I didn't
      expect my Dad to sing _all_ the verses
      of "You are So Beautiful."

EXT. PLASTECH - NIGHT

Julie and Darren approach the building cautiously.

INT. PLASTECH - HALLWAY OUTSIDE DR. HARTKE'S OFFICE

Julie and Darren round the corner to Dr. Hartke's office. When they see a janitor, CARL, on the late shift, they pull up short.

The janitor approaches a garbage can lined with a Clean bag. There's only one styrofoam cup lying on the bottom, still the janitor removes the bag and replaces it with another. He moves on.

Julie and Darren wait a beat, then move to Dr. Hartke's door. Darren fishes in his pocket for the keycard.

                    JULIE
        (whispers)
      Do you think access is restricted?

                    DARREN
      Like an alarm will sound as soon as I
      slide this card through? Only one way
      to find out--

There's a moment of suspense as Darren poises the card over the slot and then slides it through. No alarm. Just a LOUD CLICK as the door opens.

INT. DR. HARTKE'S LAB

Julie and Darren enter the lab. Julie is extremely anxious.

                    JULIE
      Just do what you need to do and let's
      get out of here.

                         DARREN
          I'm looking for the file detailing
          the composition of the Clean bags.

Darren sits down at the computer. The screen saver says
"PLASTECH." Darren hits a key on the computer.

                         DARREN (CONT'D)
          This may take a little while.

As the computer reactivates, Darren clears himself a
space. He CRACKS HIS KNUCKLES in preparation. He stares
at the screen intently. He's just about to type something
when:

A MANILA FOLDER GETS DROPPED ON THE COMPUTER KEYBOARD.
It's labelled, "CLEAN BAG -- LIST OF CONTENTS."

                         JULIE
          It's the backup hard copy. I got it
          out of the file cabinet.

                         DARREN
          Stole it the old-fashioned way...
          Good job.

Darren opens the folder to a piece of paper with the
heading: "LIST OF CONTENTS." Darren runs his finger down,
stopping at each ingredient. He sees:

#3 POLYETHELENE - 85%

POST-CONSUMER RESIN - 10%

He stops short.

                         DARREN (CONT'D)
                  (deeply disturbed)
          I knew it. There it is.

                         JULIE
          What? What is it?

Julie comes running around to look. Darren points to the
page and the word:

CHLOROPHYLLIN - 5%

                         JULIE (CONT'D)
          Chlorophyllin? Isn't that the stuff
          in plants? What's that doing in
          garbage bags?

                         DARREN
          In trace amounts, it's a pigment and
          odor-retardant. Companies put it in
          lots of products to make them green.

                    JULIE
Well, Clean bags <u>are</u> green.

                    DARREN
Yeah, but five percent is really
high. My god. Don't you get it,
Julie? Don't you see what's
happening?
          (a beat; then)
The bags are photosynthesizing!

                    JULIE
I learned about that in school.
          (that)
But forgot it.

Darren goes over to a nearby dry board to illustrate.

                    DARREN
          (he draws a plant)
A plant has leaves which trap energy
in the chlorophyll.
          (he draws a sun)
The energy is then used to make
organic compounds from the inorganic
molecules, like water and carbon
dioxide. This combined with nutrients
provided by the soil is what causes a
plant to grow.
          (he draws more leaves
           on plant)
Now with the Clickertop in place, the
Clean bag becomes a self-contained
biosphere.
          (draws the bag)
Polyethelene resin is derived from
crude oil which provides trace
nutrients like the soil does the
plants. Do you follow?

                    JULIE
Yeah. But where does the carbon
dioxide come from?

                    DARREN
From the trash. Think about it.
          (writes CO-2)
Carbon dioxide is found in things
like carbonated sodas...
          (draws soda can)
...and organic decomposition.
          (draws a little pile
           with steam)
Now once the bags are sealed, all
these inorganic molecules start
changing into organic matter. The
only thing that's missing is--

                         JULIE
          Energy from the sun.

She grabs the marker and draws more rays from the sun to
hit the bag.

                         JULIE (CONT'D)
          Which is gathered in the chlorophyll,
          completing the process and creating
          life.

                         DARREN
          That's why I couldn't get the bag to
          move this afternoon. It was raining.
          There was no sun!

                         JULIE
          Oh, god, Darren. This is a disaster.

                         DARREN
          What's the weather forecast for
          tomorrow?

Julie grabs the NEWSPAPER on Dr. Hartke's desk.

ANGLE ON WEATHER BOX

                         JULIE
          Here it is. They're predicting
          "overcast skies."

                         DARREN
          Good.

                         JULIE
               (still reading)
          "...with clouds giving way to sun
          around noon." Highs in the sixties.

They share a look then hear a noise outside the office.

INT. HALLWAY OUTSIDE DR. HARTKE'S OFFICE - NIGHT

Dr. Hartke approaches her office down the dark hall. She
stops at the door to take out her keycard. Suddenly...

A HAND REACHES OUT AND TOUCHES HER SHOULDER

Dr. Hartke jumps. She turns and sees: Carl, the janitor,
hidden in the shadows. She breathes a SIGH OF RELIEF.

                         DR. HARTKE
          Carl, you startled me.

                         CARL
          I'm sorry. I forgot how quiet it gets
          in here at night.

47

INT. DR. HARTKE'S LAB - NIGHT

Darren and Julie are frozen in fear as they listen to the voices just outside the door.

                    JULIE
               (whispering)
          What now?

                    DARREN
          We hide.

They look around. There's no obvious place.

                    JULIE
          Over there--

INT. HALLWAY OUTSIDE DR. HARTKE'S OFFICE - NIGHT

                    CARL
          You're working late.

                    DR. HARTKE
          Tomorrow's a big day for us.

                    CARL
          I haven't gotten to your office yet.
               (holds out bags)
          Do you need Clean bags?

                    DR. HARTKE
          I'm all set.

She holds up her keycard and puts it into the slot.

                    CARL
          You need anything else?

                    DR. HARTKE
          Just privacy.

She slides the card. The door CLICKS open.

INT. DR. HARTKE'S LAB - NIGHT

There's no one visible. Dr. Hartke looks around furtively, then crosses to:

A SMALL TABLE COVERED WITH A BLACK CLOTH

She looks around again, then take the black cloth off to reveal:

A FLUORESCENT PLANT LIGHT ILLUMINATING A TINY CLEAN BAG

48

Dr. Hartke examines her experiment closely. Nothing looks out of the ordinary. She takes her pen and prods the tiny Clean bag.

THE TINY CLEAN BAG SCAMPERS TO THE OTHER SIDE OF THE TABLE

                    DR. HARTKE
          It's true!

Dr. Hartke pokes the tiny Clean bag again. It scampers back to the other side. She pokes it again. It scampers again.

SFX: A LOUD CRASH FROM THE FREE STANDING METAL CABINET

Both Dr. Hartke AND the tiny Clean bag jump and turn to look at the cabinet.

INT. METAL CABINET

Julie is rubbing her elbow which clearly hit the door. She glares at Darren.

                    DARREN
               (whispers)
          Honest, I was _not_ trying to touch
          your breast.

INT. DR. HARTKE'S LAB

Dr. Hartke approaches the cabinet.

                    DR. HARTKE
          Who's in there? K-17, is that you?
          Did you escape from the other lab
          again? Bad monkey. Bad.

Dr. Hartke opens the door to the metal cabinet and Darren jumps out. Dr. Hartke SCREAMS.

                    DARREN
          Dr. Hartke, I can explain. I know
          this looks bad but I had to find out
          what was in those Clean bags. They're
          photosynthesizing. I know it sounds
          crazy and I can't prove it--

                    DR. HARTKE
          I can.

                    DARREN
          What?

                    DR. HARTKE
          I can prove it.

49

Julie emerges from the cabinet.

                    JULIE
          You believe us?

                    DR. HARTKE
          No, I believe in empirical evidence.
          When Darren came to me this morning,
          I dismissed him not because I thought
          his charge was ludicrous, but because
          his attempt to reproduce his findings
          in a lab failed. But then I started
          thinking that maybe you hadn't
          conducted your experiment under the
          right conditions, so --

Dr. Hartke leads the two over to the table with the plant
light and the tiny Clean bag.

                    JULIE
          Where'd you get the little bag?

                    DR. HARTKE
          It's a prototype for our new Clean
          sandwich sack.

                    JULIE
          It's so cute!

Dr. Hartke and Darren both shoot Julie a look.

                    DR. HARTKE
          Watch what happens under simulated
          sunlight.

Dr. Hartke once again prods the tiny bag with her pen and
it scampers across the table.

                    DARREN
          They move! I was right!
                    (then)
          This is not good. So how do we fight
          these bags?

Julie keeps POKING at the little bag with the pen.

                    DR. HARTKE
          I don't know. They don't appear to
          have any consciousness. Trying to
          reason with them would be like having
          a battle of wits with an amoeba.

                    DARREN
          An amoeba that weighs forty pounds.
          You have to do something.

                    DR. HARTKE
          I am. I'm calling Mr. Lancaster right
          now.
                    (picks up the phone)
          Julie, stop provoking the Clean bag!

Julie stops POKING. Dr. Hatke dials.

                    DR. HARTKE (CONT'D)
                    (into phone)
          Hello, Mr. Lancaster, this is Dr.
          Hartke. We have an emergency at the
          lab... You'd better come in right
          away. Yes, in your office.

INT. MR. LANCASTER'S OFFICE - A LITTLE LATER

Mr. Lancaster is sitting at his large desk. Darren, Dr.
Hartke and Julie are standing.

                    MR. LANCASTER
          ...and because of this, you want me
          to postpone the launch?

                    DR. HARTKE
          Until we perform more tests and
          figure out what exactly is going on
          with these bags.

                    MR. LANCASTER
          Out of the question.

                    DARREN
          But if you let the trucks loaded with
          the bags out into the world, it could
          devastate entire communities.

                    MR. LANCASTER
          I doubt it. We've tested these bags.
          There are a hundreds of thousands of
          them underground already.

                    DR. HARTKE
          In landfills where the sun never gets
          to them. It's the sun that triggers
          the reaction and makes them move.

                    MR. LANCASTER
          Terrific. Then you've invented the
          first bag of trash that can take
          itself out.
                    (then)
          This is ridiculous. The launch will
          proceed.

                    DR. HARTKE
          But the risk--

                    MR. LANCASTER
          (stern)
     I said, the launch will proceed.

                    DR. HARTKE
     But--

                    MR. LANCASTER
     That was your last "but," Hartke.
     You're fired. Effective immediately.

                    DR. HARTKE
     Are you kidding?

                    MR. LANCASTER
     I don't kid. And this is a good time
     to remind you that when you joined
     the company, you signed a gag clause
     prohibiting you from discussing any
     Plastech R&D for the next forty
     years. I'd think twice about shooting
     off my mouth, Dr. Hartke, or you will
     spend the rest of your life in a
     courtroom.

                    DR. HARTKE
     I'm calling the NIH.

Dr. Hartke exits. Darren turns to Mr. Lancaster.

                    DARREN
     You have no right to treat her that
     way.

                    MR. LANCASTER
     Rights? Let's talk about rights. It
     is my "right" to call the police and
     prosecute you to the full extent of
     the law for trespassing. It's even my
     "right" to shoot you and claim self-
     defense because you're on my
     property. So I'll give you a choice.

Mr. Lancaster opens a drawer on his desk and pulls out a
gun. He aims it at Darren.

                    MR. LANCASTER (CONT'D)
     You can stay on my property...
          (cocks the gun)
     or you can go.

Darren stares at him a beat.

                    DARREN
     I'll go.

                         MR. LANCASTER
Goodbye.

As Darren heads for the door, Julie follows.

                         MR. LANCASTER (CONT'D)
And where are you going, Missy?

                         JULIE
Home. It's past my bedtime.

                         MR. LANCASTER
You look familiar.

                         JULIE
I get that a lot.

                         MR. LANCASTER
You're Evan McKenna's kid.

Off Julie's look...

INT. PLASTECH HALLWAY/ELEVATORS - NIGHT

Evan, furious, is escorting Julie out.

                         EVAN
I can't believe you did this. What
were you thinking?!

He presses a button for the elevator.

                         JULIE
I was thinking about the human race.
If this national launch goes off,
within a week there'll be millions of
garbage bags smothering people all
across the country. And maybe you
don't believe me, but Dr. Hartke
does.

                         EVAN
And now she's out of a job.

                         JULIE
Is that all you can think about? Your
stupid job? Your generation is _so_
selfish.

                         EVAN
Hey, _you_ were the generation that
wore Pampers!

The doors close.

53

INT. DR. HARTKE'S LAB

Carl, the janitor, enters to start cleaning stuff up. He removes the almost empty Clean bag from the trash can and replaces it with a new one. He dusts the top of the computer, then his eye catches something.

He moves over to the tiny Clean bag which is still under the lights. The minibag QUIVERS. The plastic RUSTLES.

                    CARL
          Weird.

Carl picks up the minibag and holds it IN HIS PALM. The minibag rolls over Carl's wrist and up his forearm. Carl watches bemused, his mouth slightly open. The minibag keeps rolling over his bicep and then stops on his shoulder. The minibag is inches from his face.

                    CARL (CONT'D)
               (talking to a baby)
          Hey, whatchu doing?

THE MINIBAG LEAPS INTO CARL'S MOUTH AND DOWN HIS THROAT. Carl grips his neck. He can't breathe. He tries to stick his hand down his throat and get the bag, but he can't.

He staggers, knocking over beakers and test tubes. He FALLS TO THE GROUND.

EXT. MCKENNA'S STREET - DRIVEWAY - NIGHT

Evan and Julie are in the car. They sit in dead silence. Julie stares at the big pile of Clean bags lined up on the curb across the street as Evan pulls into their driveway.

INT. MCKENNA HOUSE

Evan and Julie enter the house in silence. Julie races to her room and slams the door.

INT. COREY'S ROOM - LATER THAT NIGHT

Corey is still playing his game. His score goes up to 3,141,593.

SFX: A KNOCK AT HIS DOOR.

                    COREY
               (still playing)
          Who is it?

                    JULIE
          Julie. Let me in.

54

Corey continues to play as he crosses to the door and unlocks it.

                    COREY
               (still playing)
          What do you want?

Julie enters and angrily sits on his bed.

                    JULIE
          I am so mad at dad.

                    COREY
               (still playing)
          Why?

                    JULIE
          Because he doesn't give a damn about
          the planet and the fact that we're
          drowning in our own garbage.

                    COREY
               (still playing)
          Don't worry about that.

                    JULIE
          Why not?

                    COREY
               (still playing)
          Because technology will take care of
          us. Technology will figure out a way
          to dispose of the garbage.

                    JULIE
          How can you be so sure of that?

                    COREY
               (still playing)
          Because technology always bails us
          out.

                    JULIE
          Maybe this time it won't.

                    COREY
               (still playing)
          You've got to have a little faith in
          science.

                    JULIE
               (getting upset)
          And what will be your contribution to
          science--the highest score in some
          stupid computer game?! Nobody wants
          to take responsibility. Your
          generation is as bad as theirs!

55

Julie exits, angry. Corey calls after her.

                    COREY
          We happen to be the same generation,
          you know!

INT. EVAN'S BEDROOM - LATER THAT NIGHT

Evan is opening the window to check his Sharper Image
WEATHER STATION. He looks at a measurement, then races
over to Gretchen's side of the bed. He nudges her awake.

                    EVAN
          Good news. The barometric pressure
          rose another half inch. I think it's
          going to be sunny tomorrow.

                    GRETCHEN
              (sleepily)
          That's great. Really great.

As Gretchen turns over to go back to sleep...

EXT. FESTIVAL GROUNDS - MORNING - OVERCAST

Workers are rolling out the rides and putting up tents. A
team of workers BEGINS TO STUFF CLAES OLDENBERG'S TWENTY-
FOOT GIANT CLEAN BAG with newspapers and hay. A worker at
the top of the scaffolding looks both ways then tosses in
a half-full styrofoam cup of coffee.

INT. HALLWAY OUTSIDE JULIE'S ROOM - LATER THAT MORNING

Evan and Gretchen are all set to go to the festival.
Gretchen KNOCKS on Julie's door.

                    EVAN
          Julie, we're heading over to the
          festival now.

INT. JULIE'S ROOM - CONTINUOUS

She is on the bed, still in her pajamas. Still angry. She
doesn't react.

                    JULIE
              (sarcastic)
          Enjoy your bloodbath--oops, I mean
          festival.

INT. COREY'S ROOM - DAY

Corey is still playing his video game. The score is now
over five million. Gretchen is standing there, arms
folded.

                    COREY
                 (still playing)
          Why do I have to go? Julie's not
          going.

                    GRETCHEN
          Julie is grounded.

                    COREY
          Why can't I be grounded?

                    GRETCHEN
          Because you haven't done anything
          wrong.

                    COREY
                 (trying)
          I've worn the same shirt for two
          weeks...

                    GRETCHEN
          Then change it and let's get going.

Corey doesn't move. He just keeps playing.

                    GRETCHEN (CONT'D)
          Okay, you have your choice. Either
          you spend one afternoon outdoors at
          the Clean Green Festival with me and
          dad or you spend two months this
          summer at the lake with Grandma and
          Grandpa where there's no electricity,
          no TV, no pizza, and no fun. What's
          it going to be?

                    COREY
          I'll pause.
                 (pauses the game)
          But I'm not going with you and Dad.
          I'll meet you there on my bike.

                    GRETCHEN
          Ten-thirty at the information booth.
                 (she starts out)
          And don't forget to change your
          shirt.

Gretchen exits. Corey pulls off his shirt and throws it
on the ground. He picks another shirt off the ground and
puts that one on. Then he goes to his bed and pulls a
suitcase out from underneath and puts it on the bed. He
opens it to reveal:

A SUITCASE FILLED WITH BOTTLE ROCKETS

                         COREY
          I'll go to your stupid festival. But
          not without the "equalizer."

Corey starts filling his backpack with bottle rockets.

EXT. MCKENNA HOUSE - A LITTLE LATER

Evan and Gretchen pull out of the driveway as Darren
watches from the bushes. As soon as the car is out of
sight, he scrambles over to the window. He climbs up the
trellis and RAPS ON JULIE'S WINDOW.

INT. JULIE'S ROOM

She turns and sees Darren at the window. She opens it.

                         JULIE
          Did my father see you?

                         DARREN
          No, they're gone.

He climbs through the window.

                         DARREN (CONT'D)
          Bad news. I spent the whole night
          trying to get the media interested in
          the bags. I called nine different
          news hotlines, but only two called me
          back, and they both said that unless
          I had videotape on the story, they
          wouldn't touch it.

                         JULIE
          There's only one way to fight that.

INT. MCKENNA HOUSE - FRONT CLOSET

Julie is rummaging through the cloest, discarding
Snackmasters, Thighmasters, Trivial Pursuit, etc...

                         DARREN
          Your family sure has a lot of stuff.

                         JULIE
                (sarcastic)
          That's why we're so happy.
                (finds a camcorder)
          Here it is!

Julie and Darren exit out the front door.

EXT. MCKENNA HOUSE

Julie and Darren are heading to the car. Julie is showing
him how to use the camcorder.

                    JULIE
          It's real easy, you just press--

                    DARREN
          Look, why don't you just show me once
          we're there?

Silence. Julie stops and looks at her feet.

                    DARREN (CONT'D)
          What? You are going with me to the
          festival, aren't you?

                    JULIE
          No. I'm sorry, but the sun is already
          starting to poke through and if the
          bags start killing people, I don't
          want to be near them.

                    DARREN
          Are you serious?

                    JULIE
               (defiant)
          We tried to warn the others and they
          ignored us. So everyone there can die
          as far as I'm concerned and that
          includes my parents and my bratty
          little brother.

                    DARREN
          I can't believe you're saying this. I
          thought we were fighting this thing.
          Together.

                    JULIE
          We were.

Julie looks down at her feet.

                    DARREN
          Man, I thought things couldn't get
          any worse...

Darren goes over to the curb and sits down with his head
in his hands. Julie puts her hand on his shoulder.

                    JULIE
          Darren--

He pulls his shoulder away. Julie looks away a the
street. A look of concern crosses her face.

                    JULIE (CONT'D)
          Darren, did you do something with the
          garbage bags on the curb?

                    DARREN
         No. It's my day off. Truck doesn't
         come through here till Monday.

SFX: A STRANGLED CRY FROM THE BACKYARD

Julie and Darren exchange a look.

                    JULIE
         Jerry--

They take off for the backyard. The gate between the
McKenna's and Jerry's property is open. Julie and Darren
run through. Julie GASPS when she sees:

JERRY SUFFOCATED BY A PILE OF BAGS AND LYING IN HIS
COMPOST HEAP

Julie starts for him, Darren holds her back.

                    DARREN
         Don't go near. They might still be
         active.

                    JULIE
         We can't just leave him there lying
         on his own compost heap!

                    DARREN
              (serious)
         Julie, he is compost now.

                    JULIE
         Oh, god. Why would they kill Jerry?
         He did everything right. He recycled.
         He had a compost heap. He was good,
         Darren. He was good.

                    DARREN
         Trash doesn't care.

Julie takes a beat as this sinks in.

                    JULIE
              (steely)
         Come on. We have a festival to go to.

EXT. CLEAN GREEN FESTIVAL GROUNDS - 9:58 A.M.

The fairgrounds are still overcast. GARY, the event
coordinator, watches as WORKERS finish stuffing the
twenty-foot Claes Oldenberg bag.

                    GARY
         Hurry, people. It's two of ten.
              (calls to a worker)
         Two of ten, Claes. Hurry, hurry.

60

One of the workers turns around, revealing himself to be
CLAES OLDENBERG.

                    CLAES OLDENBERG
          Gary, the director of the
          Philadelphia Museum did not tell me
          to "hurry" when we were installing my
          giant clothespin. We are stuffing as
          fast as we can.

                    FESTIVAL WORKER
          We're out of hay, Mr. Oldenberg.

                    CLAES OLDENBERG
          Ah, then it's done. Time to seal it
          up. The giant Clickertop, please!
                    (pointedly; to Gary)
          And take your time to get it right.

Two workers come out carrying a GIANT YELLOW CLICKERTOP.
Oldenberg goes back to supervising the art. Gary looks
miffed when Caroline approaches.

                    CAROLINE
          Gary, the big bag's spectacular.

                    GARY
                    (fuming)
          Temperamental creative types.
          Emotions flapping in the wind.
                    (looks at watch and
                     smiles)
          Ooh, it's ten. The festival's
          starting. It's starting!

Gary and Caroline run toward the entrance.

MONTAGE

MUSIC UP -- A JOHN PHILIPS SOUZA MARCH

1. EXT. PARKING LOT

The parking lot is filling up.

2. EXT. ENTRANCE TO THE FESTIVAL

There's an American flag waving next to a Plastech flag.
A banner reads, "FIRST ANNUAL CLEAN GREEN FESTIVAL."

3. INT. THE CLEAN BAG INFLATABLE FUN ROOM

Little kids (four to six-year-olds) SQUEAL WITH DELIGHT
in an inflatable jump room filled with soft-filled Clean
bags that they can jump and play in.

4. EXT. CLEAN BAG DISPLAY BOOTH

61

A crowd watches as a PRETTY DEMONSTRATION LADY wearing a low-cut dress is demonstrating "101 Uses for the Clean Bag."

> DEMONSTRATION LADY
> Number 37. Thanks to the new color,
> Clean bags even make a fabulous
> holiday gift wrap.

She holds up a box wrapped festival in a Clean bag.

5. EXT. MOVIE THEATER BOOTH -- PLASTECH WASTE THEATER

A play card announces, "Jim Carrey in Trash's Funniest Moments."

6. INT. MOVIE THEATER

On a screen is Jim Carrey doing his "Trash Man" routine. He struggles to get the bag on the can but instead puts it on his head and has to fight his way out, etc...

7. EXT. FOOD COURT - DAY

Young and old are milling about the food court, stuffing their faces with fair food--sausages and onions, lemonade, pizza, funnel cakes, popcorn and, candy apples with the Plastech logo stamped into the apple's side.

There are garbage cans lining the food court, filling up fast as can be. People are dumping greasy paper plates, cups, napkins, disposable diapers, beer cans, etc...

8. EXT. BEHIND THE FOOD COURT

The sanitation workers put Clickertop on burgeoning pile of trash bags and toss them behind the food court. A PLASTECH GUARD is nearby listening to his WALKIE-TALKIE.

> WALKIE-TALKIE
> (with static)
> ...all clear in sector 28.

The guard notices two bigger kids racing to jump on the pile of Clean bags. He stops them with his arm.

> PLASTECH GUARD
> Where do you think you're going?

> BIGGER KID
> To play in the bags.

> PLASTECH GUARD
> You're not allowed back here. This is
> REAL garbage.

62

EXT. MIDWAY -- INFORMATION BOOTH

Evan is eating cotton candy. Gretchen takes one more bite out of a candy apple and THROWS HERS AWAY, HALF-EATEN.

                    GRETCHEN
              (notices a spot on
               her white jacket)
         Oh, darn. I got sticky stuff on my
         jacket.

                    EVAN
         Why did you wear white to a fair
         anyway?

                    GRETCHEN
         They said it was a "Clean" festival.

She grabs a BUNCH OF NAPKINS from a nearby concession stand and starts dabbing at the stain. From behind, they hear a voice.

                    COREY
              (breathing hard)
         Mom... Dad...

They turn and see Corey hanging over the handlebars of his bike. The physical exertion was a lot for him.

                    EVAN
         Champ, you made it.

EXT. MIDWAY - A LITTLE LATER

Evan, Gretchen and Corey walk along the midway. Gretchen is looking at a pamphlet: "Plastech: Making Things Better."

They pass an ARCHERY SITE where people are shooting arrows into Clean Bags that are filled and have bullseyes painted on them.

                    GRETCHEN
              (pointing at archery)
         I want to do that later. I was pretty
         good at archery in camp, you know.
         And there's a three-legged race at
         noon. I thought you and I would enter
         that, eh, Corey?

                    COREY
         I think it would be more fun for you
         and Dad to do.

                         EVAN
          I can't do it at noon. I have to go
          meet Mr. Lancaster and the Board of
          Directors up at Plastech.

                         GRETCHEN
          Then it's you and me in the three-
          legged race.

Corey rolls his eyes as they pass A WOMAN CARRYING CLEAN
BAGS FILLED WITH HELIUM SO THEY LOOK LIKE BALLOONS

                    HELIUM BALLOON LADY
          Get your Clean bag balloons! Clean
          bag balloons here!

EXT. FESTIVAL PARKING LOT - DAY

Darren pans the fairgrounds with the camcorder. Through
the camera lens we see families playing, a mother pushing
a stroller, grandparents handing cotton candy to a
grandchild. People are happy.

                    DARREN (V.O.)
          Here we are at the first, and
          probably last, annual Clean Green
          Festival. I'm Darren and this is
          Julie.
               (turns the camera)
          Julie, do you have anything to say to
          the people at home about the
          approaching Armageddon?

                    JULIE
               (on camera)
          Yes. When you live in the suburbs
          everything seems so safe and boring
          that you keep hoping something weird
          and exciting will happen. And now
          that it has...
               (a beat, then)
          I just wish I could go back to
          feeling safe again.

A SCREAM IN THE DISTANCE

Julie and Darren whip around worried that it's begun.

ANGLE ON A YOUNG GIRL ON THE FERRIS WHEEL

The girl SCREAMS because she's stuck at the top of the
wheel with a brother who is rocking the carriage wildly.

EXT. BEHIND FOOD COURT - DAY

The security guard watches as Plastech sanitation workers
continue to ADD TO THE GROWING PILE OF BAGS.

                    PLASTECH GUARD
                 (into walkie-talkie)
          ...The trash pile is growing faster
          than we expected. We're going to have
          a problem on our hands.

EXT. FESTIVAL MIDWAY - DAY

Evan, Gretchen and Corey are watching a GUY JUGGLE THREE
LARGE TRASH BAGS. Evan hears a voice behind him.

                    MAYOR NANCY (V.O.)
                 (stern)
          Plastech just doesn't know when to
          stop. As Mayor of Newfield, I should
          shut this place down.

Evan turns, concerned.

                    MAYOR NANCY
                 (breaks into a smile)
          I mean, you just give and give and
          give to this town.

Evan breaks into a SMILE OF RELIEF and warmly greets
Newfield's forty-year old MAYOR who is wearing a Plastech
baseball cap and t-shirt and is loaded with freebies.

                    EVAN
                 (relieved)
          Mayor Nancy. Welcome to the Clean
          Green Festival.

Gretchen self-consciously covers the stain on her white
jacket.

                    GRETCHEN
          I see you got some Clean bag samples.

                    MAYOR NANCY
          Just stocking up, now that they've
          decided to stop giving them to us for
          free.

She shoots a jokingly angry look at Evan.

                    EVAN
          We've got to start charging for the
          bags some time, Mayor. How else are
          we going to make a little money for
          the company?

                    MAYOR NANCY
          You know what I say, what's good for
          Plastech is good for Newfield.

65

Just then, Mayor Nancy's twin girls, KIKI and KATIE (13) come by. They both clearly have a crush on Corey.

                    GRETCHEN
          Hello, Kiki and Katie. Corey, you
          know Mayor Nancy's twin girls, don't
          you?

                    MAYOR NANCY
          Sure, he does. They're in the same
          grade.

                    KIKI
               (moves closer to
                Corey)
          Hi, Corey.

                    KATIE
               (moves closer to
                Corey)
          Hi, Corey.

                    COREY
          Um... yeah.

It's too much for Corey, who takes a step back.

                    EVAN
          Come on, son, you can be a little
          friendlier.
               (whispering)
          For god's sake... they're twins!

                    GRETCHEN
          It's time we headed over to the three-
          legged race.
               (to Mayor Nancy)
          Can you join us?

                    KATIE/KIKI
          Yes!/Let's go!

                    COREY
          I'll see you there.

Panicked, Corey rushes off on his bicycle.

                    EVAN
               (calls out)
          Good luck, Corey. Make your dad
          proud.
               (to Mayor Nancy)
          I've got to head up to corporate HQ
          for a meeting.

66

> MAYOR NANCY
> Give Mr. Lancaster my best. Will he
> be stopping by the festival?

> EVAN
> I'm sure he'll try. You know there's
> nothing he loves more than hanging
> out with the folks of Newfield.

INT. PLASTECH -- CORPORATE DINING ROOM - DAY

Fourteen men in suits and ties and one woman (the BOARD
OF DIRECTORS) are enjoying a SPECTACULAR BUFFET
(lobsters, filet mignon, shrimp, etc...) in a beautiful,
windowed room on the top floor of Plastech which
OVERLOOKS the fairgrounds. Butlers pour champagne.

HARRY STARKLEY is helping himself to heaping spoonfuls of
caviar. He shoves a toast point loaded with Beluga into
his mouth just as Mr. Lancaster approaches.

> MR. LANCASTER
> Enjoying yourself, Harry?

Harry struggles to swallow the big bite. Some black fish
eggs remain in the corner of his mouth.

> HARRY STARKLEY
> This is the most delicious caviar
> I've ever had in my life. Bet it was
> pretty expensive.

> MR. LANCASTER
> You have about two hundred dollars
> worth on your plate. And another
> fifty on your tie.
>   (Harry reacts)
> But we'll just keep that between you
> and me. The stockholders don't need
> to know that.

> HARRY STARKLEY
> If Clean bags are as effective as you
> say, they won't care.
>   (he laughs; spitting
>   caviar by mistake)
> Whoops. I just spit out twenty bucks.

Mr. Lancaster reacts.

EXT. FESTIVAL - THREE-LEGGED RACE - DAY

Corey and his mother are tied at the middle leg with a
strip of Clean plastic to show its durability. Corey
looks absolutely miserable.

67

Kiki and Katie are next to them also tied together, creating a bizarre Siamese twin effect. There are various other participants. Mayor Nancy is at the starting line with the starter's pistol.

                    MAYOR NANCY
          On your mark. Get set. Go!

The contestants take off! Gretchen is going at a fast clip. Corey starts to pant. He tries to slow down, but Gretchen is working hard to keep up the pace.

                    COREY
          Slow down. Mom.

                    GRETCHEN
               (truckin')
          Huh?

                    COREY
          Slow down.

                    GRETCHEN
          This is too fast for you?

The twins pass them. Corey is really hurting.

                    COREY
               (breathing hard)
          Yes.

                    GRETCHEN
          It can't be.

                    COREY
          It is. It is. I can't...

Corey collapses, taking his mom down with him. The twins turn to see. They LAUGH at him. Corey angrily unties himself from his mom. He grabs his backpack and stalks off. His mother calls after him.

                    GRETCHEN
          Corey...

                    COREY
          Leave me alone.

He STARTS TO RUN, but after a few steps has to SLOW DOWN to a fast walk because his lungs can't take it.

EXT. RANGER STATION - DAY

Corey is HUFFING and PUFFING as he struggles to climb the ranger station. He gets to the top and lies down. From that position, he UNZIPS his backpack to reveal the BOTTLE ROCKETS.

68

EXT. BEHIND FOOD COURT - DAY

The pile of bags is now HUGE AND UNCONTAINABLE.

                    PLASTECH GUARD
               (into walkie-talkie)
          ...we've already reached maximum
          capacity. We can't take it anymore.
          The bags are out of control.

As some bags start to roll off the top...

EXT. ATOP BONE HILL - DAY

Albie is sitting among several tied Clean bags. He has
just finished his lunch and he leans against a bag to
take a nap. A gentle breeze blows. The clouds begin to
break. The sky begins to brighten. Albie hears the noise
of a CLATTERING TRASH CAN and sits up. He sees:

A BEAM OF SUNLIGHT FALLING ON A BAG. THE BAG BEGINS TO
SHAKE.

                    ALBIE
               (sleepily)
          It's happening...
               (wide awake)
          It's happening! I must warn the
          others.

Albie jumps up and starts down the hill. As he runs, the
bags he was leaning against begin to SHAKE. They take off
after him.

Five bags are following Albie. He looks back. A bag
leaves the pack and picks up steam, rolling past him.

                    ALBIE (CONT'D)
          Get away from me!

The bag stops right in front, causing Albie to trip. He
rolls down the hill and ends up flat on his back.

POV: ALBIE'S FACE

He is lying on the ground. His eyes open. He tries to get
up and can't.

ALBIE IS PINNED ON ALL FOUR LIMBS BY BAGS

He THRASHES and SCREAMS and STRUGGLES, but he's no match.
Slowly the fifth bag approaches his face.

                    ALBIE (CONT'D)
          No. Please, no. NOOOOOO!

69

Albie's scream is muffled as the bag jumps on his face and SMOTHERS HIM. The bag jumps off. Albie is still breathing a little. Now the bag is toying with him. It jumps back on Albie's face. His body convulses. And then lies still.

The bag rolls off and sets down the hill. The other bags follow. Albie is left, motionless, on the hill.

EXT. FESTIVAL - BAND STAND - DAY

The band is set to play. One of the band members takes the microphone.

                    LEAD SINGER
          Well, it looks like the sun decided
          to make an appearance after all.

A band member plays the first four notes of "Here Comes the Sun."

                    LEAD SINGER (CONT'D)
          Well, that's enough about the
          weather. It's time to rock and
          roll!!!

They start playing.

EXT. BEHIND THE FOOD COURT

The HUGE PILE OF BAGS IS BATHED IN SUNLIGHT. The unsuspecting security guard finishes making the last plans he will ever make.

                    PLASTECH GUARD
               (into walkie-talkie)
          ...Moving these bags to sector
          thirty. Copy that.

He looks over at the bags and sees them SHAKING. They start to TUMBLE and ROLL. The guard is confused. As he talks, a group of Clean bags form A CIRCLE AROUND HIM.

                    PLASTECH GUARD (CONT'D)
               (into walkie-talkie)
          What the hell--? It looks like the
          bags are moving themselves... No, I'm
          not nuts. This is the creepiest thing
          I've ever seen. You better alert
          security that-- hey, stop laughing...
          Come on, I'm not joking!...

The circle is complete. The guard is starting to sweat. He whips his head to the right and sees he is SURROUNDED BY BAGS. He whips his head to the left. Same thing. They have built a crater around him and are slowly filling it in.

                    PLASTECH GUARD (CONT'D)
              (into walkie-talkie)
          They've got me surrounded! You'd
          better--

A CLEAN BAG LAUNCHES ITSELF. It FLIES at the guard,
KNOCKING THE WALKIE-TALKIE OUT OF HIS LEFT HAND.

                    PLASTECH GUARD (CONT'D)
          That's enough.

The guard PULLS HIS GUN. Another bag FLIES at his right
hand, KNOCKING THE GUN OUT. Then the circle begins to
close in. THE BAGS GET CLOSER AND CLOSER.

EXT. MIDWAY - DAY

People start putting on sunglasses.

ANGLE ON THE CLEAN BAG BALLOON LADY

The helium-filled bags start jerking around on their
strings. The balloon lady reacts, confused. She struggles
with them. They drag her along the ground until she lets
go.

ANGLE ON THE HELIUM-FILLED CLEAN BAGS RELEASING INTO THE
SKY

INT. CLEAN BAG INFLATABLE FUN ROOM - DAY

The kids are jumping up and down in the bags. Parents
watch, smiling.

                    TIMMY
          Mom, Dad--look at me! Look at me!

Timmy gets SWALLOWED BY THE BAGS. His parents watch
smiling a beat, then look at each other concerned when
Timmy doesn't resurface. Timmy's head pops out.

                    TIMMY (CONT'D)
              (screaming)
          Help!! Help!!

He gets sucked under again. Timmy's dad rushes over to
the "Fun Room" and starts to climb in. The operator takes
notice.

                    FUN ROOM OPERATOR
          Sir, you're too big to go in there.

                    TIMMY'S DAD
          The hell I am.

Timmy's Dad climbs in and immediately gets SWALLOWED UP.

71

EXT. LANDFILL SHAFT - DAY

Remember how workmen had to open up a trench in the landfill? Now sunlight is seeping into the PIPE and a LASER BEAM hovers about SIX INCHES from where the pipe meets a subterranean MOUNTAIN OF CLEAN BAGS.

EXT. MIDWAY - DAY

People are screaming. Sanitation workers are running after rolling bags. Rolling bags are running after sanitation workers. "Bag-ettes" are fleeing.

EXT. FESTIVAL PARKING LOT

Darren is holding the camcorder, taping the mayhem.

                    DARREN
          Just like we thought.

                    JULIE
          Let me see, let me see.

Darren hands her the camcorder. She focuses in on the action.

POV: CAMCORDER

                    JULIE (CONT'D)
          My god. Those people don't stand a
          chance.

The camcorder zooms in on:

GRETCHEN COMING OUT OF THE MOVIE THEATER

Gretchen looks around confused. A bag brushes past her. Then another. She starts to run away. They follow her.

                    JULIE (CONT'D)
          Mom...!

Julie drops the camcorder and starts running.

                    DARREN
          Julie, where are you going?

                    JULIE
          My mom's in trouble.

Darren takes off after her.

EXT. FESTIVAL - SACK RACE -DAY

The race has just begun with people in Clean bags hopping along. Bags start rolling toward the people and they start hopping faster.

72

A SEVEN-YEAR OLD FRECKLED BOY is leading the race and really picks up pace when he sees the bags behind him. He crosses the finish line and keeps going toward the landfill hill.

INT. PLASTECH - CORPORATE DINING ROOM - DAY

Mr. Lancaster, Evan and GRAYSON DEAN, a distinguished director, are standing around the buffet, congratulating each other.

> GRAYSON DEAN
> You've outdone yourself, Lancaster. A national launch getting off right on schedule. That's unheard of.

> MR. LANCASTER
> We have McKenna to thank for that. Without him, the Clean bag would still be in the development stage.

> EVAN
> That's nice of you to say, sir, but everyone at Plastech deserves credit.

> MR. LANCASTER
> Forget the team play. You're the one responsible for all this.

Evan glows.

EXT. FESTIVAL - MIDWAY - DAY

There's garbage everywhere. Julie and Darren are clawing at a pile of bags, trying to dig Gretchen out from underneath.

> JULIE
> Mom, hold on. We're almost there.

Julie and Darren finally tear open the last bag, revealing GRETCHEN PASSED OUT, lying in the garbage slime. Julie feels her neck.

> JULIE (CONT'D)
> (panicking)
> She's not breathing.

> DARREN
> Mouth to mouth.

Julie cleans the muck that's been forced into her mom's mouth:

> JULIE
> Oh, god, what's this goo?

73

Julie attempts resuscitation.

> DARREN
> (under his breath)
> Come on. Come on.

Anxious moments. Is it too late?

GRETCHEN GASPS FOR AIR AND OPENS HER EYES

> JULIE
> Mom.

> GRETCHEN
> Julie.
> (then)
> What--?

> JULIE
> I'll explain later.
> (to Darren)
> Tell the others to split open the
> bags. It's the only way to stop them.

Gretchen looks down at her slime-covered white jacket.

FRECKLED BOY

The freckled boy in the sack is still hopping up the hill
toward the landfill opening.

LANDFILL SHAFT (ON THE OTHER SIDE OF THE HILL)

Sunlight has moved further down the trench, now it's
three inches away from the SUBTERRANEAN MOUNTAIN OF CLEAN
BAGS.

EXT. FESTIVAL - THE BAND STAND

Darren has jumped up to the band stand. He grabs the
microphone.

> DARREN
> Listen to me, people. You have to
> pierce the skin of the bag. If you
> break the seal, it stops the chemical
> process. Do whatever it takes. Break
> that seal.

MONTAGE - PEOPLE BATTLING THE BAGS

1. People run by a WEENIE ROAST to grab forks, which they
use to stab the bags.

2. The BAG-ETTES take off their high heels and rip the
bags apart with them.

74

3. OMAR climbs up a tree and thinks he's safe. The bags start to stack themselves one on top of another until they reach him. He kicks at the column of bags.

> OMAR
> Go away! Go away!

The bags try to knock him off the tree. It looks like they will succeed. Then at the last second, a BOTTLE ROCKET comes flying out of nowhere and rips the bags open.

EXT. RANGER STATION - DAY

Corey is looking through a pair of binoculars and trying to help people out.

> COREY
> Man, that would have been worth about a thousand points.

EXT. MIDWAY - DAY

4. A garbage bag is on top of someone when Darren comes roaring up on a motorcycle with Julie behind him holding a BOW AND ARROW that she picked up from the ARCHERY CONTEST. Julie lets arrows fly while Darren steers.

ANGLE ON FRECKLED BOY

Still hopping, the freckled boy nears the top of the hill.

ANGLE ON LANDFILL SHAFT

The sunlight is half an inch from the bottom of the shaft.

ANGLE ON THE BURNING SUN

The sunlight moves about a quarter inch more.

SFX: THE SUNLIGHT HITS THE BAGS

The bags start to TREMBLE in the subterranean cavern. They begin to move around like excited molecules. The sun continues to hit them through the shaft like a laser beam. The bags get more and more FRENZIED.

THE FRECKLED BOY

Still in the sack, the freckled boy reaches the top of the hill. He looks back at the town and breathes a SIGH OF RELIEF. He turns and sees:

THE SIDE OF THE HILL TREMBLING

75

The freckled boy's eyes get large. The hill keeps trembling and shaking, until:

THE HILL ERUPTS LIKE A GIGANTIC JIFFY POP

The ground falls away and A MILLION CLEAN BAGS start pouring out. There are more bags than you can imagine. More bags than there were zombies in "Night of the Living Dead." More bags than you could ever poke. And they just keep coming and coming and coming.

The freckled boy starts running back towards the festival.

                    FRECKLED BOY
          Hey, everyone! Hey--

The cute, freckled boy trips on his sack and falls over. He looks behind him and sees the STAMPEDE OF BAGS. Within moments, he is TRAMPLED TO DEATH.

EXT. BEHIND THE FOOD COURT

The PLASTECH GUARD is lying on the ground. His WALKIE-TALKIE CONTINUES TRANSMITTING.

                    WALKIE-TALKIE
               (with static)
          Come in, sector twenty-eight. Come
          in.

Darren and Julie come riding up on the motorcycle. Julie hops off the motorcycle and feels for a pulse in his neck.

                    JULIE
          We're too late!

                    DARREN
          Grab the walkie-talkie.
               (she does)
          Let's head back to the midway. I
          think we're starting to contain the
          bags.

As Julie starts to get on the bike, she looks in the opposite direction. Her face changes. She's scared.

                    JULIE
          Darren.

                    DARREN
          What?

                    JULIE
          You'd better look over there.

76

Darren turns and sees:

THOUSANDS OF CLEAN BAGS COMING OVER THE HILL

Darren reacts, super-calm.

                    DARREN
          Get your mom. The battle's over.
          We've got to get to high ground.
               (re: walkie-talkie)
          And let them know we need help.

                    JULIE
               (into walkie-talkie)
          Come in. Can you read me. The bags
          are going nuts. They're all over the
          place. We're all going to die!

EXT. MIDWAY - DAY

The stampede of bags is fast approaching. As the first
wave hits, PANIC DOUBLES. Mayor Nancy grabs the twins and
starts running toward the parking lot which appears safe.
Bags are nipping at their heels. The twins are crying.

                    MAYOR NANCY
          Run, twins, run!

EXT. PARKING LOT - DAY

Mayor Nancy and the twins just make it into the car. They
lock their doors as the bags leap at the windows. Mayor
Nancy fumbles with the key in the ignition.

          KIKI   KATIE
I want to go home!   I don't like this!

Mayor Nancy puts the key in the ignition and STARTS the
car. She puts it into DRIVE and... nothing. The car won't
move. Nothing appear to be wrong (no bags in sight) so
she opens the door and looks underneath.

UNDER THE CAR

The whole area is tightly packed with bags so the car
can't move. In fact, all the cars are packed with bags
underneath. Mayor Nancy quickly closes the car door.

                    MAYOR NANCY
          Twins, it's time to pray.

More and more bags roll in, filling up the parking lot.

77

INT. PLASTECH - CORPORATE DINING ROOM

The Board of Directors happily applaud as a CHEF WHEELS
IN A BIG CAKE IN THE SHAPE OF A GARBAGE BAG. Evan stands
next to a smiling Mr. Lancaster.

                    MR. LANCASTER
          As soon as our man in charge cuts the
          cake, we'll head down to the loading
          bay and watch the trucks roll out.

The Board of Directors applaud some more. A guard enters
holding a walkie-talkie. He approaches Mr. Lancaster.

                    PLASTECH GUARD #2
          Sir, we're getting some strange
          transmissions from the festival.
          There seems to be some trouble.

Mr Lancaster doesn't drop his smile.

                    MR. LANCASTER
               (to Evan)
          You handle it.

Evan takes the walkie-talkie from the guard.

                    PLASTECH GUARD #2
          I've got the volume on low. There was
          some crazy lady screaming into it.

As Evan turns the volume up:

                                        INTERCUT WITH:

EXT. THE HILL LEADING TO THE RANGER STATION - DAY

Julie, Darren and Gretchen are heading up the hill.
Gretchen is holding the walkie-talkie.

                    GRETCHEN
               (hysterical; into
               walkie-talkie)
          ...We tried to stop them, but there
          are too many. The Jensens are dead.
          And so is Mrs. Murphy. It's only a
          matter of time before they come after
          us. Help! Help!

INT. PLASTECH - CORPORATE DINING ROOM

                    EVAN
               (into walkie-talkie)
          Honey, is that you?

                    GRETCHEN (V.O.)
          Evan? Evan, help! It's horrible!!

                         EVAN
                  (into walkie-talkie)
         I will. Now calm down...

Board members start to look at Evan oddly. Evan tries to
shield the walkie-talkie from view.

                         GRETCHEN (V.O.)
         You calm down! The kids were right.
         It's happening. The bags are killing
         people!

                         EVAN
         Gretchen, where are you?

EXT. JUST BELOW THE RANGER STATION

                         GRETCHEN
         Below the ranger station.

                         EVAN (V.O.)
         And where are the kids?

                         GRETCHEN
         Julie and Darren are with me. But,
         Evan, I don't know where Corey is--

                         EVAN (V.O.)
         What?!

                         GRETCHEN
         I lost him in the--

Julie is up ahead. She turns and yells back.

                         JULIE
         Mom! Mom! Corey's up here!

Gretchen scrambles up to the ranger station and sees
Corey.

                         GRETCHEN
         My baby!

                         EVAN (V.O.)
         You found Corey?

                         GRETCHEN
         He's here. And he's fine.
                  (Corey shoots off a
                   bottle rocket)
         And he's shooting off bottle rockets.

                         EVAN (V.O.)
         Dammit! I told him he could only use
         those under parental supervision. Let
         me talk to him.

                        GRETCHEN
          You can yell at him later. Right now
          we need you to--

INT. PLASTECH - CORPORATE DINING ROOM

                      MR. LANCASTER
          Cut the cake, McKenna. Cut the cake.

Evan is startled to see Mr. Lancaster offering him a
knife. The Board of Directors looks on expectantly. Evan
looks extremely embarrassed.

                         EVAN
          Now is not a good time, Mr.
          Lancaster.

                      MR. LANCASTER
          I beg your pardon?

                         EVAN
          There's a complication I'm trying to
          handle right now.

Grayson Dean steps in.

                      GRAYSON DEAN
          Is something wrong?

                      MR. LANCASTER
          No. Everything's fine.
               (tightens his grip on
                the knife)
          Isn't that right, McKenna?

Evan stares at him a beat. Before he can answer:

                      HARRY STARKLEY
               (looking out the
                window)
          Hey, how come bags are piling up
          outside the building? Is that part of
          the promotion?

The Directors rush to look outside the windows. Clean
Bags have rolled down from the landfill and are piling up
outside of Plastech.

                       LEN TUCKER
          That doesn't look right to me.

                     IRVING SPELLMAN
          Or me.
               (to Lancaster)
          Hey, what's going on?

                    GRAYSON DEAN
          Yeah. What's going on?

As the Board of Directors AD-LIB, "What's going on?" DR.
HARTKE BURSTS THROUGH THE DOOR.

                    DR. HARTKE
          I'll tell you what's going on. We've
          created a monster. And the people
          down there are fighting a war.

                    HARRY STARKLEY
          Against what?

                    DR. HARTKE
          Against everything we've ever thrown
          away!

                    MR. LANCASTER
          Don't listen to her. She's crazy. And
          fired. I don't even know how she got
          past our security system.

                    DR. HARTKE
               (in your face)
          I designed it, okay?
               (to Directors)
          There's no time to lose. You can see
          the bags piling up outside the
          building. We must dismantle the
          machines that make them and destroy
          the inventory.

                    HARRY STARKLEY
          But what about the launch?

                    DR. HARTKE
          There won't be any launch! The bags
          are killing people!

                    GRAYSON DEAN
          Perhaps we should think about
          postponing.

                    IRVING SPELLMAN
          A week couldn't hurt.

                    HARRY STARKLEY
          What's a week?

The Board of Directors start to AD-LIB agreement when Mr.
Lancaster steps in and regains control.

                    MR. LANCASTER
          That's enough! There will be no
          postponement. The Clean bags will be
          launched.
                    (MORE)

                    MR. LANCASTER (CONT'D)
          (to Dr. Hartke)
Who the hell are you to decide what
the consumer wants and doesn't want?
          (to Board)
Who the hell are we. We're just here
to provide them with options.

                    DR. HARTKE
But these bags are dangerous. We have
to protect people.

Mr. Lancaster grabs a package in a nearby display.

                    MR. LANCASTER
There's an eight-hundred number on
the side of the package. If there are
any problems, people will call and
we'll deal with them on a case-by-
case basis.

                    DR. HARTKE
          (shaking her head)
I can't believe you're not going to
do anything about this. You really
don't care.

                    MR. LANCASTER
I do care. I care that the launch
goes ahead on schedule.
          (to the room)
Now if you'll excuse me. I'm going to
the men's room.

Mr. Lancaster exits. There's a beat of silence, then:

                    HARRY STARKLEY
And that's why he's president and CEO
of the corporation.

The Board of Directors all break into LAUGHTER OF RELIEF.

                    DR. HARTKE
          (to Evan)
You're not going to let him push this
through?

                    EVAN
What can I do?
          (off her look)
I'll talk to him when he gets back.
          (off her look)
I'll go talk to him now.

Evan heads out.

INT. PLASTECH - HALLWAY OUTSIDE THE EXECUTIVE WASHROOM - DAY

Evan approaches the door marked "Executive Washroom." This is REALLY HARD. Finally, he KNOCKS.

                    EVAN
              (to door)
         Don't worry, sir. I'm not coming in.
         I just wanted to talk. It's me,
         McKenna. I agree we should launch on
         schedule. But first let's run down
         into the field and see these bags in
         action. If it looks bad, maybe we
         could delay. Not postpone, but DELAY.
         I don't believe that's asking too
         much. Thanks for hearing me out.

Evan presses his ear against the door. Nothing. He gets suspicious. He puts his hand on the knob and throws it open.

THE WASHROOM IS EMPTY.

Lancaster gave him the slip! Evan runs down the hall.

INT. CORPORATE DINING ROOM - DAY

Evan enters and sees the Board of Directors and Dr. Hartke staring aghast out the window.

SFX: HELICOPTER NOISES

Evan enters in time to see Mr. Lancaster give them all the "thumbs up" before flying away in his corporate helicopter.

                    DR. HARTKE
         He's saving his own butt!

                    EVAN
         I don't believe it!

                    LEN TUCKER
         What do we do now?

All eyes turn to Evan. The moment of truth.

                    EVAN
         End this.

INT. PLASTECH HELICOPTER - DAY

The chatty pilot sits in the cockpit while Mr. Lancaster sits in the body of the helicopter in a big leather chair, looking at the CARNAGE BELOW.

                    HELICOPTER PILOT
          Where to today, sir?

                    MR. LANCASTER
          The cabin upstate.

The pilot flicks a few switches. Mr. Lancaster sits back
and picks up a newspaper. Because the pilot is wearing
HEADPHONES, he speaks a little LOUDER than normal.

                    HELICOPTER PILOT
          So today's the big launch?

                    MR. LANCASTER
               (not looking up)
          Uh huh.

                    HELICOPTER PILOT
          You must be excited.

                    MR. LANCASTER
               (not looking up)
          Uh huh.

                    HELICOPTER PILOT
          I know nothing about the business,
          but I really think these Clean bags
          will take off. They're so strong. I
          use 'em like suitcases, you know?
          See.

The pilot reaches down under the co-pilot's empty chair
and pulls out a filled Clean bag. He places it on the
seat next to him--THE SUN HITS IT.

                    HELICOPTER PILOT (CONT'D)
          Maybe you could use that in an ad. I
          could give a testimonial about how
          much traveling I do and how I'm
          always on the go an--

                    MR. LANCASTER
               (finally looks up)
          Do you mind?...
               (sees the bag)
          Dear god, what's that doing there?

                    HELICOPTER PILOT
          Or I could say "Clean bags are
          "taking off" just as I'm "taking
          off."

Mr. Lancaster tugs at his seat belt. It won't undo.

                    MR. LANCASTER
          The sun...

84

The bag starts to VIBRATE.

                    HELICOPTER PILOT
          Or I could say something about how
          strong the bag is--

THE BAG KNOCKS THE PILOT OUT WITH ONE SHOT. The pilot
slumps to the side. The helicopter starts jerking around.
The Bag covers the controls. Lancaster finally gets his
seat belt undone and lunges into the cockpit. He
struggles to rip the bag away from the control panel. The
helicopter is unstable. Lancaster finally tears the bag
away. Clothes and toiletries tumble out. Mr. Lancaster
reaches for the controls to try and right the copter and
looks up.

THE COPTER IS RIGHT IN FRONT OF A TRANSMITTER TOWER

Mr. Lancaster's eyes register his doom, then:

FX: HELICOPTER CRASHES AND EXPLODES

INT. PLASTECH LOADING BAY - DAY

Dr. Hartke, Evan, the Board of Directors and a dozen
truck drivers are throwing cartons of Clean bags off one
of the six trucks in a bucket-brigade style. The truck is
almost empty. There are five other trucks in the bay that
are loaded and ready to roll. As Evan hands a carton down
the line:

                    EVAN
          Last one.

                    DR. HARTKE
          Okay, everyone into the truck.

The Board of Directors race to get into the trucks,
except for Harry Starkley who is on a cell phone off to
the side of the dock. Dr. Hartke approaches him.

                    HARRY STARKLEY
               (into phone)
          ...I said dump the Plastech. Every
          share I've got. Dump it. Dump it.
          Dump it.

                    DR. HARTKE
          Mr. Starkley--

                    HARRY STARKLEY
               (into phone)
          You heard me? I gotta run.

MOMENTS LATER

85

Evan closes the truck's trailer door sealing the directors and teamsters in safely. He locks the door and walks around to where Dr. Hartke is standing by the driver's seat.

                    DR. HARTKE
          We can't put it off any longer. We
          need to decide which one of us stays
          behind, turns on the gas and torches
          this place.

A beat as both contemplate this weighty decision.

                    EVAN
          I think it should be me. I've always
          convinced myself that the reason I
          work so hard for Plastech is to
          provide for my family. Well, here's a
          chance to <u>really</u> do something for my
          family.

                    DR. HARTKE
          Are you sure? I invented the bags.

                    EVAN
          But I marketed them.
               (re: walkie-talkie)
          At least, I'll get to say goodbye.

Evan starts off, holding the walkie-talkie.

                    DR. HARTKE
          Maybe there's some other way...

                    EVAN
          There isn't. For the first time in a
          long time, I can see what's right and
          wrong. And I'm going to do what's
          right.

                    DR. HARTKE
               (calls after him)
          You're a good man, Evan McKenna.
               (then)
          Could you hit the garage door on your
          way out?

Evan hits a red button. Slowly, the garage door starts to open as Dr. Hartke gets in the truck,

DR. HARTKE REVS THE ENGINE

As the garage door rises, the THOUSANDS OF CLEAN BAGS that were piling up along the Plastech building start rolling in. They've been waiting for an opening and now they've got it. Dr. Hartke determinedly shifts the truck into gear and starts to drive.

86

As the truck heads out, bags roll under it, making it hard for the truck to move. Dr. Hartke presses the gas pedal all the way to the floor. The TRUCK LURCHES AND BARRELS THROUGH THE PILE OF BAGS.

EXT. RANGER STATION - DAY

Gretchen is on high ground. Safe. For now.

                    GRETCHEN
               (into walkie-talkie)
          You volunteered to what?!

                    EVAN (V.O.)
          Honey, these could be my last few
          minutes on earth. I really don't want
          to spend them fighting with you.

                                   INTERCUT WITH:

INT. PLASTECH LAB - DAY

                    EVAN
               (into walkie-talkie)
          I love you. I always have. I hope you
          know that.

                    GRETCHEN
          I do. And I love you.

                    EVAN
          Now let me talk to Julie.

                    JULIE (V.O.)
               (through walkie-
               talkie)
          Hi, Dad, it's me.

Evan opens a cabinet filled with jars of alcohol. He unscrews the tops and start pouring it on the floor.

                    EVAN
          Julie, I'm glad I have the chance to
          say this: you were right. I'm sorry I
          didn't listen to you earlier. Boy, am
          I sorry.

                    JULIE (V.O.)
               (getting emotional)
          Daddy, I wish I hadn't been right.

                    EVAN
          Don't cry. You have to be strong for
          your mother. I love you, sweetheart.
          Remember that always. Now put Corey
          on.

                    COREY (O.S.)
              (through walkie-
               talkie; flat)
          Hi, Dad. What do you want?

                    EVAN
          Nothing. I guess I just wanted to
          say...
              (this is difficult)
          I'm sorry I never played baseball
          with you, son.

                    COREY (V.O.)
          That's okay. I never wanted to.

Evan rips the tubes out from some nearby Bunsen burners,
and then twists the nozzles.

SFX: THE GAS HISSES OUT OF THE JETS

Evan eyes the fume hood and the duct work leading to the
wall.

                    EVAN
          You be a good boy. Take care of your
          mom. And don't shoot off any more of
          those bottle rockets.

                    COREY (V.O.)
          I won't.

                    EVAN
          I mean that now, you hear? They
          really could do some damage.
              (lightbulb)
          Wait. Do you still have any left?

                    COREY
          One. But I'll break it right now.

                    EVAN
          No, don't! You're at the ranger
          station, aren't you? I bet you could
          set off this explosion by sending one
          through the window.

                    COREY
          It's pretty far.

                    EVAN
          But you could do it. Look--

Evan goes to the lab window and opens the Venetian
blinds.

                    EVAN (CONT'D)
          Can you see me?
               (waves)
          I'm waving in the window.

EXT. RANGER STATION - DAY

They see a tiny Evan waving like an idiot from a
distance. They all wave back like idiots.

                    EVAN (V.O.)
               (through walkie-
                talkie)
          Now you see the vent above me?

Evan points to the vent above where the gas duct leads.

                    EVAN (V.O.)
          All you've got to do is sail a bottle
          rocket in there. You got that?

                    COREY
          Yeah, okay.

Evan studies the switch on the hood and turns it on. The
vent fans ROAR.

INT. HARTKE'S LAB - DAY

Evan has a cloth covering his mouth. He COUGHS AGAIN.

                    EVAN
          I've got to get out of here. Wait for
          my signal.

He exits the lab, coughing.

EXT. BONE HILL ROAD TO RANGER STATION - DAY

Dr. Hartke drives the truck up the road to the ranger
station.

                    DARREN
          Dr. Hartke--

She pulls the truck to a stop and jumps out of the cab.

                    DR. HARTKE
          What's going on?

                    GRETCHEN
          Evan's on his way out! Corey's going
          to send a bottle rocket in that vent.

Gretchen points. Dr. Hartke looks and panics.

                         DR. HARTKE
          That vent? That tiny vent? You think
          he can hit a target of that size with
          pinpoint accuracy?

                         GRETCHEN
          He's my son. I love him. I trust him.
          And, frankly, I think it's the only
          thing he CAN do.

Corey start lining up his shot. He frowns. Something's
missing. He holds up his left hand.

                         COREY
          You know this would be a lot easier
          if I had a pop can to balance me.

                         JULIE
          I'll get you one.

Julie spots a pile of discarded trash (candy wrappers,
beer cans, and cigarette boxes) in the nearby bushes. She
heads down the ranger station.

INT. PLASTECH STAIRWELL - DAY

Evan is heading down the Plastech stairs.

                         EVAN
                    (through walkie-
                    talkie)
          Honey, you still there?

                         GRETCHEN (V.O.)
          Yes. And so's Dr. Hartke.

                         DR. HARTKE (V.O.)
                    (through walkie-
                    talkie)
          Hi, Evan.

                         EVAN
          Hey, Hartke! Looks like I didn't have
          to be noble after all!

EXT. RANGER STATION - DAY

                         DR. HARTKE
          Yeah, but you have to be fast. That
          gas has to be ignited within four
          minutes of exposure or the automatic
          flow control will activate the
          sprinklers and we'll never blow the
          lid off that sucker.

                         EVAN (V.O.)
          It started flowing over a minute ago.

> DR. HARTKE
> I'll start the countdown at three
> minutes

Dr. Hartke gets her digital watch at 3:00. It clicks down to 2:59 in just a second.

> DR. HARTKE (CONT'D)
> Can you get out in time?

INT. PLASTECH STAIRWELL - DAY

> EVAN
> I think so. So far, the coast is
> clear. I don't see any bags.

> DR. HARTKE (V.O.)
> Where are you?

> EVAN
> The stairwell.

> DR. HARTKE (V.O.)
> Good. It's nice and dark in there...

Evan turns a corner to descend the final staircase.

> DR. HARTKE (V.O.)
> (remembers)
> Except for the basement skylight!

Sure enough, sunlight is streaming in, hitting the bottom of the stairs. About twenty bags are at the bottom, teetering. Evan freezes in his tracks.

> EVAN
> (hushed and panicked)
> They're here.

> DR. HARTKE (V.O.)
> Don't make any sudden moves. Do you
> understand? No sudden moves.

CLOSE UP of Evan flexing his hand around the stair railing. That's all it takes. THE BAGS POUNCE.

> EVAN
> Arghhh!

EXT. RANGER STATION - DAY

Gretchen grabs the walkie-talkie from Dr. Hartke.

> GRETCHEN
> Evan! Evan!

                         EVAN (V.O.)
                    (through walkie-
                    talkie)
          They're all over me!

The walkie-talkie goes dead. They all exchange looks.
Darren starts to move down the hill.

                         DARREN
          I'm going in there.

                         DR. HARTKE
          No! There isn't time. We have to blow
          the place up in...
                    (checks her watch)
          ...a minute, fifty-nine.

                         COREY
                    (protesting)
          I'm not shooting a bottle rocket
          while my dad's still in there.

                         DR. HARTKE
          Corey, you don't have a choice.

                         COREY
                    (turns to Gretchen)
          But, Mom...

                         GRETCHEN
                    (what to do?)
          Oh, gosh, Corey. I think this thing
          may be bigger than just our family.
          It's the fate of the world...

Corey starts to shake. He can barely even hold the bottle
rocket.

                         DR. HARTKE
          Pull yourself together. Minute,
          thirty-four.

                         COREY
          I can't. I won't.
                    (into walkie-talkie)
          Dad! Dad!

INT. PLASTECH STAIRWELL - DAY

The walkie-talkie has been knocked onto a stair. Although
it cannot transmit, voices still come through.

                         COREY (V.O.)
                    (through walkie-
                    talkie)
          Can you hear me, Dad?!

92

A pile of twenty bags lies still at the bottom of the stairs. Evan is nowhere in sight.

> DR. HARTKE (V.O.)
> (through walkie-
> talkie)
> Corey, it's hopeless. His walkie-
> talkie is dead. He's probably dead.

> COREY (V.O.)
> (through walkie-
> talkie)
> No!

> GRETCHEN (V.O.)
> (through walkie-
> talkie)
> Sweetheart, get a grip.

> COREY (V.O.)
> (through walkie-
> talkie)
> I want my dad. He can't be dead. Dad.
> Dad!

The BAGS START TO TREMBLE. STRANGE NOISES come from inside, then:

A HUMAN HAND HOLDING A SWISS ARMY KNIFE BURSTS THROUGH. The arm is covered in garbage. EVAN'S HEAD FOLLOWS.

> EVAN
> Yaaaaaaah!

He has cut his way out! He GASPS FOR AIR. He hears the walkie-talkie.

> DR. HARTKE (V.O.)
> Corey, you have to take aim. We're
> down to under a minute.

Evan scrambles for the walkie-talkie and grabs it.

> EVAN
> (into walkie-talkie)
> Hello? Do you read me?

They don't.

> GRETCHEN (V.O.)
> (insistent)
> Shoot it!

> DR. HARTKE (V.O.)
> Forty seconds.

93

Evan THROWS THE BUSTED WALKIE-TALKIE AWAY. He races to the stock room.

INT. PLASTECH STOCK ROOM

The room is stocked with boxes of Clean bags. Evan runs to the door leading to the loading bay and looks through the window in the door. He sees:

THE LOADING BAY IS FILLED WITH BAGS

                    EVAN
          How the hell do I get out of here?

EXT. RANGER STATION

Dr. Hartke is reading off her watch.

                    DR. HARTKE
          Thirty. Twenty-nine.

Julie runs over, holding a discarded pop can.

                    JULIE
          Look, Corey, I got you a pop can.
               (she forces it into
                his limp left hand)
          Now, come on, you can do this.

                    DR. HARTKE
          Twenty-three. Twenty-two.

                    GRETCHEN
          She's right. Make us proud.

                    DARREN
          Make your dad proud.

This gets Corey's attention.

                    DR. HARTKE
          Nineteen. Eighteen.

                    COREY
               (sniffles)
          I'll try.

Corey raises the bottle rocket and aims it for the vent. He is breathing hard. He wipes some sweat off his brow. Julie and Gretchen take hands. Darren puts his arm around Julie.

                    GRETCHEN
               (under her breath)
          Come on, Corey.

                    DR. HARTKE
          Twelve seconds.

                    PLASTECH GUARD
          Don't hurry him!

                    DR. HARTKE
                 (under her breath)
          Ten. Nine. Eight.

Corey takes final aim. He fumbles in his pocket a beat
and then takes out a lighter. He IGNITES THE FLAME.

                    DR. HARTKE (CONT'D)
          ...four. Three.

Corey shifts his weight, squints his eyes.

                    DR. HARTKE (CONT'D)
          Two.

                    COREY
                 (screams)
          D-a-a-a-a-d!

COREY SENDS THE BOTTLE ROCKET FLYING

It SCREAMS through the air and HITS ITS MARK. The bottle
rocket sails through the narrow vent, then:

BOOM!

DR. HARTKE'S LAB EXPLODES!

MR. LANCASTER'S OFFICE EXPLODES!

THE STORE ROOM WITH CARTONS OF CLEAN BAGS EXPLODES!

THE LOADING BAY WITH THE TRUCKS EXPLODES!

EXT. RANGER STATION - DAY

Gretchen, Corey, Julie, Darren and Dr. Hartke watch as:

PLASTECH EXPLODES IN A HIGH, BILLOWING FLAME

The group at the ranger station duck and cover. Debris is
scattered. A FEW SHABBY BAGS ROLL ONTO THE HILL.

When it calms down, they all look at each other. This is
no cause for celebration. Corey stares frozen at what
used to be a building. Gretchen pats Corey on the
shoulder to console him. Julie sobs quietly as Darren
holds her.

Just then, one of the SCATTERED BAGS STARTS TO SHAKE.
PLASTIC RUSTLES. IT SHAKES MORE. THE BAG IS STILL ALIVE.
THEN A HAND TEARS THE BAG AWAY TO REVEAL:

EVAN! HE LIVES!

                    COREY
          Dad!

The family REJOICES. Evan climbs out of the bag.

                    EVAN
          I escaped! They thought I was one of
          them!

Evan rushes to hug his family. As he embraces each one.

                    EVAN (CONT'D)
               (to Gretchen)
          Sweetheart.
               (to Julie)
          I'm sorry I doubted you.
               (to Corey)
          Kickass shot. There is nothing this
          family can't do when it sticks
          together!

The family celebrates. Julie beams.

                    EVAN (CONT'D)
               (to Darren)
          And I suppose you want to date my
          daughter now...

Everyone is still smiling when Dr. Hartke steps in.

                    DR. HARTKE
          The danger's not over, folks. There
          are still about half a million bags
          running around Newfield.

Indeed, BAGS ARE ROLLING across the countryside,
aimlessly maneuvering their way through what's left of
the fair.

                    GRETCHEN
          Do you think they'll start mating?

                    DR. HARTKE
          Who knows? We know so little about
          them.

                    DARREN
          We'll never be able to fight this
          many.

                              JULIE
                    (gets an idea)
          I know. We'll wait until it gets dark
          and then we can run around and poke
          all the bags easy, no sweat.

                              EVAN
          Great idea.

                              DR. HARTKE
          We can't wait. We need absolute
          containment immediately.

          But how--

                              DR. HARTKE
          I don't know. I don't know.

                              COREY
          Then we're doomed. There's no way
          out.

                              GRETCHEN
                    (pointing)
          What's that?

They all look up at the sky.

                              DARREN
          Looks like the birds.

EXT SKY - DAY

A SEAGULL CRUISES DOWN FROM THE SKY. IT DIVES INTO A BAG
AND BUSTS IT OPEN.

SFX: SEAGULLS CHIRPING

Seagulls start coming in droves and tearing at the bags
with their beaks.

EXT. PARKING LOT

Mayor Nancy and the twins are still trapped in the car,
which is being shaken by the bags. The car is surrounded
except for a tiny sliver of window. Through it, Mayor
Nancy sees the SEAGULLS SWOOPING DOWN.

                              MAYOR NANCY
          Twins. Twins. The birds are coming to
          save us.

More birds follow. They tear at the bags. Bags try to
ROLL AWAY but they're no fast enough.

MORE SEAGULLS

97

Everywhere, seagulls are swooping down and tearing at garbage bags.

EXT. RANGER STATION - DAY

The tiny group rejoices.

                    JULIE
          The birds are doing it! They're
          attacking the bags!

Dr. Hartke opens the back of the truck. The Board of Directors come out.

EXT. FESTIVAL - DAY

Darren, Julie, Gretchen Evan, Corey, and Dr. Hartke and the Board of Director rejoin the festival armed with sticks. They stab at any bags that the birds haven't destroyed.

                    HARRY STARKLEY
               (jabbing with his
                stick)
          Ha! Ha!

The festival slowly comes back to life. People are coming out from under trash cans and getting out of the Zipper cars, and climbing down from trees. There are still bags around. Everyone is giddy.

Mayor Nancy and the twins run in, having escaped from the car.

                    MAYOR NANCY
          We're winning! The town is winning.

All of a sudden, both twins point.

                    KATIE
          Hey--

                    KIKI
          --look!

THE GIANT CLAES OLDENBERG BAG IS STARTING TO SHAKE.

                    MAYOR NANCY
          Holy--

It's not over. People SCREAM. The birds are no use against the giant bag.

THE BAG STARTS TO BARREL DOWN THE HILL.

ANGLE ON JULIE AND DARREN

98

Julie looks at Darren. He has a plan.

                    DARREN
          I'll be right back.

He runs up alongside the giant bag.

                    DARREN (CONT'D)
          Over here. Over here. Take me.

Darren veers off away from the crowd. The Claes Oldenberg
bag follows him at a fast clip. To stay in front, Darren
has to run all out. Julie and the others watch nervously.

Darren glances back. The Claes Oldenberg bag is gaining
on him. He tries to run faster. A carton of greasy
popcorn is in his path. Darren doesn't see it.

Darren TRIPS and falls to the ground hard. He turns and
sees the Oldenberg bag getting closer. It's looming right
in front of him. It's about to crush him! Darren looks
desperately for something--anything--to stop it.

A METAL SIGN ON A STEEL POST IS LYING ON THE GROUND

Darren spots the sign. And just as the Oldenberg bag
starts to fall on him, he rolls out, grabs the pole, and
braces it against the ground. The bag falls on him.

SFX: A GIANT TEAR

The steel rod has pierced the Oldenberg bag. The stuffing
falls all around Darren who breaks into a smile as he
realizes he is saved. He looks over at the metal sign on
the ground and for the first time reads its message:

"PLEASE DISPOSE OF TRASH PROPERLY"

Darren LAUGHS IN RELIEF. Off to the side, we see:

THE CAMCORDER LYING ON THE GROUND TAPING DARREN.

FX: THE IMAGE TURNS INTO THE TV NEWS

The camera pulls back to reveal ANCHORWOMAN TRICIA
GARRITY. The shot of Darren and the scene is frozen
behind her.

                    TRICIA GARRITY
          Today's tragedy ended as bizarrely as
          it began. In the end, it was nature
          that saved the people of Newfield.
          The birds swooped in and made the
          world right again. And if I may
          editorialize, I think we all learned
          something today.
                    (MORE)

                    TRICIA GARRITY (CONT'D)
          I think we all learned that in the
          future--if there's going to be a
          future--man had better reduce
          packaging and learn how to work with
          nature not against nature.

A HAND REACHES IN AND TURNS THE TV SCREEN OFF

INT. MCKENNA'S KITCHEN - THAT EVENING

It was Gretchen's hand. She and Evan were watching on the
small kitchen TV. Gretchen starts to wipe the counter
while Evan enjoys a mini sandwich snack.

                    GRETCHEN
          Tricia Garrity has gotten so preachy
          these days.

Gretchen comes across the mini-sandwich package on the
counter and tosses it into the garbage can. Evan SNATCHES
it out of the air. As he places it on the table:

                    EVAN
          I think maybe I'll call the eight-
          hundred-number later and tell them
          there's a consumer out here who
          doesn't like the way this thing is
          packaged. So wasteful.

Julie and Darren enter the kitchen.

                    JULIE
          If it's okay with you guys, we're
          going to a movie.

                    GRETCHEN
          It's fine. Have fun.

                    EVAN
          And don't worry about bringing her
          home at any time. I know she's safe
          with you.

Darren and Julie share a look.

                    GRETCHEN
          On second thought, have her back by
          midnight.
               (they start out)
          Oh, Julie, before you go, have you
          seen your brother?

                    JULIE
          I saw him head into his room.
          Probably back playing those computer
          games.

INT. COREY'S ROOM - EVENING

Corey is holding his remote control and staring at the
computer screen where his game is on pause. He hasn't
starting playing again.

A moment of truth. Corey puts the remote down, walks to
the side of the computer and...

COREY FLIPS COMPUTER SWITCH OFF.

The screen goes black. Corey grabs TWO DUSTY BASEBALL
MITTS and a baseball from a shelf. He smiles and as he
heads out of the room.

                    COREY
              (calling out)
         Hey, Dad!

EXT. BONE HILL - EVENING

The sun is just starting to set behind the hill. There's
a slight breeze. The camera pans skyward. It's going to
be a beautiful evening. The sky is a brilliant sapphire.
There's not a cloud in sight. All is still except for...

ONE HELIUM-FILLED CLEAN BAG BALLOON FLOATING ALONG WITH
THE BREEZE.

                    THE END

Join the Secret Script Vault Fan Club

Now that you've reached the end… shall we continue
this awesome journey together?

<u>Yes, let's do it!</u>

*Do you think reading scripts is cool and you want to be the
first to know when we release more?*

*Would you like to see the script you just read made into a
movie/TV show?*

*Would you enjoy hearing our writers talk about their work and
share funny, behind the scenes stories?*

Join the Secret Script Vault fan club for free at our website!
You'll be the first to hear about everything we do with your
favorite writers, including our podcast and events. We love to
surprise and delight our fans. We can't wait to meet you!

Join the fan club now at:

www.SecretScriptVault.com

Founder, Secret Script Vault

Kaia Alexander

Nell Scovell is a comedy writer and author of *Just the Funny Parts: And a Few Hard Truths about Sneaking into the Hollywood Boys' Club*. She was the creator/showrunner of ABC's *Sabrina, the Teenage Witch* and has written for *The Simpsons*, *Monk*, *Charmed*, *Late Night with David Letterman, NCIS*, and *The Muppets*.

Joel Hodgson started out performing magic and ventriloquism in eighth grade and went on to create Mystery Science Theater 3000 in the late '80s. The show is still going strong with over 200 episodes and a Peabody Award for Excellence in Broadcasting. Also, its latest iteration on Netflix is rated at "100% Fresh" on Rotten Tomatoes. As a performer, Joel has appeared on *Saturday Night Live*, *Freaks and Geeks*, and voiced the role of Mayor Dewey on the animated series *Steven Universe*.